BASIC AND ADVANCED
LIGHT PLANE MAINTENANCE

Firewall Forward —Maintaining Power

The Light Plane Maintenance Library
Volume Four

BASIC AND ADVANCED
LIGHT PLANE MAINTENANCE

Firewall Forward —Maintaining Power

By the Editors of *Light Plane Maintenance* Magazine

Belvoir Publications Inc.
Riverside, Connecticut 06878

ISBN: 0-9613139-1-9

Contents

Part III: GETTING THE MOST ENGINE LIFE

Preface

It can be argued (with some justification) that the aircraft engine's "bottom end"—i.e., the crankcase, crankshaft, camshaft, accessory section, etc. (everything except the cylinders)—is among the least-understood parts of a modern light plane. Even experienced pilots tend to remain mum when the talk turns to con rods, bearing caps, and oil pump impellers. And yet, it is essential for a pilot to know what these things are, if any contemplation is being given to TBO-busting, for example, or operation at the limits of performance. When it comes to firewall-forward components, knowledge is indeed power.

This volume in the *LPM Library* series is, in effect, a companion to the very first volume in the series, *FWF: The Top End*. As such, it is intended to broaden the pilot's understanding of firewall-forward phenomena *other* than those involving valves, pistons, and cylinder barrels. Knowing how the top end works is only the first step in understanding what makes the engine function. In this volume, you'll gain a greater understanding of engine trouble signs, TBO risk factors, cold-weather considerations, inflight troubleshooting, and what to do in case of overspeed or sudden stoppage (e.g., a prop strike). You'll go beyond the basics of everyday engine operation and learn how to evaluate inflight roughness, high oil consumption, low power, poor break-in, and a variety of other problems. You'll also learn how to protect your engine in cold weather—as well as in times of inactivity.

The present volume is one of very few books to address the subject of modern light plane turbocharging: how it works, how AiResearch and Rajay turbos differ in design, how wastegates function, how controllers differ. The tricky subject of automatic controllers (and how they work to prevent overboosting) is dealt with in comprehensive detail, yet in language simple enough for any high-school student to understand. The mysteries of intercooling are also addressed—and attendant myths laid to rest.

The section on major overhaul will prove useful to any owner/operator contemplating an engine rebuild. Included is a highly technical, detailed list of 20 questions to ask your overhauler before you send your engine in for teardown. Attention to the questions in this list

may save many dollars, and many agonizing hours of troubleshooting and warranty wrangling, down the road.

The propeller governor isn't generally thought of as a power-train component per se; and yet, it literally governs the power output of the engine (on planes with constant-speed props). In design, the modern prop governor resembles nothing so much as a conventional oil pump, and to achieve its function it uses actual crankcase oil. Hence, it is very much a part of the engine, and a complete discussion of the constant-speed, single-acting (CSSA-type) governor is therefore included in Chapter 6.

Finally, in the Appendix to this volume is a section on EGT (exhaust gas temperature) analysis. EGT systems have, over the course of the past 25 years, become an integral part of the instrument panel of high-performance piston aircraft and have proven their worth many times over in troubleshooting situations (to say nothing of their value for mixture management). Ironically, however, few engine instruments are as widely misunderstood as the modern EGT (or "exhaust analyzer," as it is sometimes called). The technical excellence of *LPM's* past articles on EGT technology (and its application) is reflected in the definitive introduction to EGT interpretation that follows the last chapter to this book.

Our hope is that this will be viewed as a unique book—unique not only in its arrangement of subject matter, but in its contribution to pilot education as well. Aviation has long needed a no-holds-barred technical guide to the operation and care of air-cooled, opposed engines, written not in the legally sanitized argot of the manufacturers' handbooks, but in the evenhanded, caring manner of one pilot writing to another. If we've managed to convey that sort of subject treatment here, we'll have judged our efforts worthwhile.

Good luck, and happy flying!

The Editors of LPM
Riverside, Connecticut

Prologue

Shoddy engine maintenance has a way of catching up with people. What you don't pay for now, you invariably pay for later.

Take the case of N4700E, a 1969 Aero Commander 680FL which flew cancelled checks for Purolator Corp. up until September 1980. On September 3, 1980, Commander 4700E made its final flight. Taking off from Chicago's Midway Airport shortly before 5:00 in the morning, the pilot of the heavily loaded plane radioed the tower (less than a minute after brake release) that he wanted to come back to land. Seconds later, the pilot said "can't hold it . . ." and the aircraft crashed in a residential area, burning on impact.

Several "witnesses" who heard the plane fly over their houses described the plane's noise as that of a single-engine aircraft. A truck driver who actually saw the impact said that the plane's engine "was missing and backfiring occasionally." The plane was observed to make a prolonged, steep left turn prior to impact. Neither propeller was feathered.

The National Transportation Safety Board laid the probable cause of the crash to "material failure" of the number-five-cylinder exhaust valve seat of the plane's left engine. (The seat came loose and wedged in the exhaust port, hanging open the exhaust valve.) "With the exhaust valve open," the Board concluded, "no power is produced from the cylinder, and a large drop in RPMs results."

The Board also faulted the pilot for not taking proper action to avert an accident. The NTSB report on the crash contains a lengthy discussion of accelerate-stop distances, takeoff abort procedures, etc., indicating that the Safety Board clearly believed the pilot knew of the power loss early enough in the takeoff to abort safely. (That the pilot knew this is not all evident from existing data, however.)

Could the loss of one valve seat, by itself, down a heavily loaded (but still 300 pounds under gross) Aero Commander? Does it make sense that the hanging open of one exhaust valve could so rob a twin-engined airplane of power that it crashes out of control? After all, in an engine with six cylinders, you would expect the loss of one exhaust valve to mean, at most, the loss of one-sixth of the engine's rated power—right?

Wrong. In the case of the Aero Commander 680FL, which is powered by six-cylinder Lycoming IGSO-540-B engines rated at 380 horsepower each, the loss of one cylinder's output can mean a loss of far more than 16.6 percent of the engine's power. The reason has to do with the way supercharging works. In the IGSO-540, takeoff power comes at 47 inches of manifold pressure and 3,400 rpm. The high manifold pressure is achieved by means of a mechanical supercharger driven off the crankshaft. If the takeoff manifold pressure of 47 inches could be maintained following the hanging open of one cylinder's exhaust valve, the remaining five cylinders would indeed put out their normal takeoff power, and the engine would lose, overall, just one sixth of its total power. But what actually happens is that when one cylinder loses power, less crankshaft torque is available to turn the supercharger impeller—and some of the 47 inches of manifold pressure are lost. What's more, since the intake valve to the "bad" cylinder is open about one-third of the time—and since the "bad" exhaust valve is open *all* the time—a large portion of the remaining manifold pressure will be dissipated out the faulty jug. This in turn degrades the output of the "good" cylinders even further.

So it's actually easy to see how the loss of one exhaust valve seat, in one cylinder of a supercharged six-cylinder engine, can lead to the loss of much of the engine's total horsepower—perhaps half or more.

Still, if full takeoff power was available from the remaining (good) engine, why did N4700E fail to maintain altitude after losing, say, half of the power from its left engine?

The plane may have lost altitude due to pilot actions (attempting a steep turn back to the field, for instance). In N4700E's case, however, it seems likely that the plane's inability to maintain altitude on the "good" engine may have been due to the fact that the remaining engine was anything but good.

At 8:30 p.m. the night before the accident, attorney John Juergensmeyer was at Bloomington Airport in Bloomington, Illinois, waiting for ground transportation. (Juergensmeyer had just completed a flight with his pilot-associate Rick Jakle in the company Seneca.) "I was inside and heard the girl at the desk speaking on the phone," Juergensmeyer recalls. "I later learned she was talking to the control tower. 'Was the pilot aware that he had flames coming from his engine?' she said. She was looking at a plane sitting immediately ouside. I walked out to observe." Mr. Jakle was already out front, gesturing with crossed hands to the pilot of the plane in question, and pointing at the plane's right engine. The plane was Aero Commander N4700E.

"The right engine was opposite me and I could not see it," Juergensmeyer continues. "Jakle later commented that *flames had been bursting from the engine exhaust.* The pilot (of 4700E) shook his head and waved at Rick; Rick shrugged his shoulders and moved aside, and the pilot taxied away.

"The engine noise was extremely rough, with occasional popping and erratic acceleration. The plane waited a while for the runway to be clear. Rick commented to me, 'Watch this carefully—it may be your only chance to see an engine-out on takeoff.' In the background, a hangar resident, who I later learned was named Oliver Luersson, was commenting that he had been flying for 40 years and would never take off in a plane with an engine that rough. We watched the airplane closely as it took off in darkness, and as full power was applied the engine noise became more regular and the takeoff appeared to be made without incident."

The 29-year old pilot of 4700E, in his last pre-crash "squawk memo," had complained of several maintenance glitches, most notably fuel-flow problems with the right engine. Fuel flow was "above redline during cruise"; further, the "engine would not shut down properly." The pilot told of having to advance the throttle several times on shutdown to get the right engine to quit. Cylinder head temperature problems (overheating) were also cited.

Avco Lycoming performed teardown audits of each of the Aero Commander's engines in the presence of FAA and Safety Board witnesses. The left engine had been overhauled by Schneck 761 hours prior to the accident; the right engine had 549 hours SMOH (overhauler unknown). Neither engine was in particularly good shape, maintenance-wise. (The maintenance records were incomplete, but it was apparent that several cylinders and at least one magneto had been changed in the field since the time of overhaul.) The airplane's "good" engine (the right one) contained not a single cylinder with compression better than 40/80 (although after staking the valves, two jugs came up to 70/80). Also, the left mag on the right engine was found finger-tight. Inexplicably, no teardown analysis of the right-engine fuel injector system was done.

Amazingly, despite the low compression (and other discrepancies), Lycoming—in its final teardown report on N4700E's power-plants—judged each engine to be "in essentially normal condition for the reported operating time."

Maintenance records for the plane showed that N4700E had (in the12 months prior to the crash) seen repair of exhaust leaks with stainless-steel tape, "cleaning and gapping" of spark plugs to correct mag roughness, use of WD-40 at the control pedestal to correct stiff prop controls, etc. Rather than comply with AD 80-09-10 on heater inspection, the plane was placarded "Do not use heater." Maintenance was not (to put it mildly) of the "spare no expense" variety—although it isn't clear whether this was the result of policies laid down by the plane's owners, or by Clark Aviation of Bloomington, IL (the maintaining agency).

That the exhaust valve seat fell out of cylinder number five of N4700E's left engine is clear from Lycoming's teardown report. Exactly *why* or *how* the seat fell out was never determined, however. According to the NTSB's final report, "The exhaust valve seat for No. 5 cylinder, left engine, shows it was loose in the recess for a time before it started moving up and down with the valve. High temperature, such as application of takeoff power, can cause the valve seat to fall out of the recess and slip behind the valve head."

In any event, the lesson of N4700E's last flight should be clear. There's nothing worse, when the chips are down, than altitude above you, runway behind you, and maintenance dollars sitting unspent in the bank. Remember that as you read the chapters that follow.

Part I

ANTICIPATING TROUBLE

Chapter 1

LOOKING FOR FWF DISTRESS

Today's engine prices being what they are (outrageous), aircraft owners—and potential owners—have become more concerned than ever about determining the state of an engine's health (or ascertaining the need for a top or major overhaul). Many pilots wonder if there is an easy way to do this—by monitoring oil consumption, say, or perhaps cylinder compression (or whatever).

The fact is, there is no simple, easy way to keep tabs on an engine's health because no *one* technique is foolproof. The key is to combine *different* techniques.

Although oil consumption and cylinder compression are favorite tools for making snap judgments of an engine health, one can easily

get into trouble using these measurements. Oil consumption varies tremendously from engine to engine depending not only on engine model, but on operating conditions, ambient temperatures, grades of oil used, and many other factors (including, of course, the condition of the piston rings, valve guides, and bearings).

What's "normal" for one engine type and one operator may or may not be acceptable for another engine type or operator. Maximum allowable oil consumption rates are shown in the operator's handbooks and/or overhaul manuals for various powerplant models. On engines of 400 cubic inches or larger, maximum allowable oil usage is almost always over one quart per hour. Anything less than that is, by definition, acceptable.

Similarly, although many operators assume that cylinder compression scores tend to downtrend over the life of an engine—and although the FAA has arbitrarily chosen 60/80 as a minimum acceptable compression reading (see AC43.13-1A, par. 692)—the fact is that [1] cylinder compression readings tend to yo-yo up and down over the jug's life and [2] for a variety of reasons, a cylinder that shows less than 60/80 compression can actually be 100% sound mechanically and materially, as either of the engine manufacturers will tell you. Also, [3] compression scores are exceedingly sensitive to engine temperature, operator technique, and equipment calibration. A single compression reading, or set of readings for one engine, is meaningless, by itself.

A single measurement, of any kind, usually tells you exactly nothing. What you want to monitor are data *trends*. Is oil consumption increasing, or decreasing? Is cylinder compression steadily going up, or down? More important still, *can you correlate the oil-usage trend with the cylinder compression trend, and/or other relevant data?*

What might "other relevant data" consist of? Oil spectrum analysis is often helpful, as is visual analysis of used oil-filter elements. (Don't skip one in favor of the other. What shows up in oil analysis may not show up in the filter, and *vice versa*.) Visual inspection of spark plug firing ends is also a good way to get to know an engine—but once again, you have to be careful. If several spark plugs are black with oil (obvious misfirers), ask yourself: Are they misfiring because they're oily with oil escaping past the compression rings? Or are they oily *because they're misfiring* (due to lead deposits, connector-well flashover, a harness defect, or some other unrelated phenomenon)?

Getting to know an engine takes time. It takes a hundred hours or more to build a *data baseline* that you can work away from when it

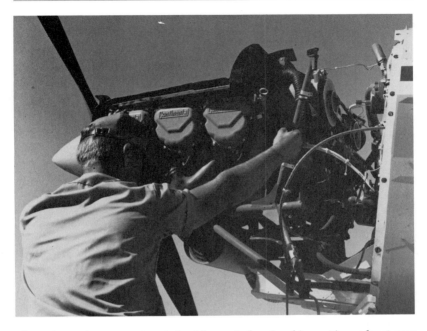

The entire engine compartment should come in for visual inspection at least once every 25 hours, with particular attention to engine mounts, exhaust system, control connections, and fluid lines.

comes to judging oil analysis reports, oil consumption patterns, etc. Nonetheless, there are some "quick" ways to get a handle on an engine's state of health, if, for instance, you are evaluating a strange airplane for possible purchase. We recommend the following:

Carefully measure the dipstick oil level before and after a one-to-two-hour flight, making sure the plane is on level ground both times, and allowing at least a 10-minute drainback period after engine shutdown. (If oil analysis is to be performed, aspirate oil via the filler neck *after* the engine is flown. Note the time since last oil change.)

Load the aircraft to near gross, take off, and note the plane's sea-level rate of climb at Vy. (Take density altitude into account. If need be, observe the rate of climb at increments of 1,000 feet, plot the rates on a graph versus density altitude, and extrapolate back to sea level, to get an idea of the plane's real-world performance at sea level.) Compare your numbers with the book figures. Unless the airframe has been modified in some obvious way, the numbers should be very close. If not, you're looking at a weak engine.

Some engines are more tightly cowled than others. This Mooney's Lycoming O-360 has specially fitted cooling baffles that form a "cowl within a cowl." Top spark plugs are inside the cooling shroud.

Again at gross weight, climb to altitude and make a full-throttle speed check. If you're more than 5 mph or 4 knots away from book speeds (taking ASI calibration errors into account, naturally), you may be looking at a weak engine.

Continue to fly at high power settings for an hour or more. Keep an eye on oil pressure readings throughout the flight. If oil pressure is high at initial level-off at cruise altitude, but significantly lower after an hour of cruising (perhaps even down around the low end of the green arc), make a mental note of it—particularly if it's a cold day. Low oil pressure in the winter means no oil pressure in the summer.

After landing, keep low-power operation to a minimum. Taxi to the ramp as quickly as possible, shut the engine down, and remove the top-hole spark plugs. After an hour or more of high cruise, if any of the top plugs is oily and black, you can suspect ring wear in the cylinders of origin.

The most important thing to remember is: Don't rely on any *one* indicator to tell you how strong (or how worn out) an engine is. It takes more than one data point to draw a curve—or a conclusion.

LOW POWER

Failure to deliver normal power is an insidious, hard to pinpoint condition that afflicts almost every piston-engine aircraft sooner or later. Often the cause can be located quickly (via EGT indications, for example). Many times it cannot, however. The question is, what can the pilot do then, other than turn the keys to the ship over to the shop?

First, it's important to realize that static rpm is affected dramatically by air temperature, barometric pressure, wind, oil temperature, air filter condition, etc. (to say nothing of tachometer calibration) so that day-to-day variations in full-throttle rpm are inevitable, in a fixed-pitch plane especially. (Static rpm will not equal actual takeoff rpm, in any case.) Read your shop manual, POH, or engine operators' manual to find the static rpm limits for your engine, and bear in mind that those limits do not take density altitude into effect.

If your engine is low on power, you'll notice it primarily in rate of

The Lycoming O-235-L (seen here on the firewall of a Piper Tomahawk) is a solid-tappet engine and thus sensitive to valve lash adjustment. Improper lash, a leaky carb heat door, lead-fouled spark plugs, and/or the wrong magneto timing can cause low power output.

climb. (This is true regardless of tachometer calibration error.) The airplane's Vy rate of climb at full gross should be within 10 percent of book (as measured via stopwatch and altimeter).

Also, you should be able to reach the published service ceiling, fully loaded, and still have a positive indication on the VSI. (Make allowances for density altitude.)

When it is clear that normal power is not being delivered, check easy things first. The carburetor heat door should open/close fully, with no leaks; check that the control knob has some "cushion" at the panel. (A carb heat control that hits the panel isn't rigged properly.) The same considerations apply to alternate air, in injected aircraft.

The "control cushion" check should be made for mixture and throttle as well. The mixture and throttle arms should be hitting their stops at the carburetor or injector before the cockpit controls hit the panel.

Visually check the air filter and (with the filter removed) the airscoop for obstructions. FAA has received reports of some new paper filters being clogged with excess glue (faulty construction), so even new filters should be checked.

Carburetor or injector overrichness/overleanness is easy to check: Note the rpm rise when the mixture is retarded at idle, and also at runup rpm. A rise of 50 to 75 rpm is acceptable; more than 75 rpm increase indicates an overrich condition. (If no rpm rise is seen during the runup leanout, slowly apply carburetor heat with the mixture full rich. Any increase in rpm with the initial application of carb heat indicates an overlean condition.)

In an injected engine, the takeoff fuel flow should be within the limits set in the appropriate manufacturer's engine operating handbook or service manual. A too-high flow indication on a pressure-type panel gage may indicate nozzle clogging or a maladjusted injector or fuel pump.

Perform a magneto check at 2,000 rpm (or as advised in your owner's manual). Rpm dropoff on each mag should not exceed 175 rpm, nor should the difference between mags be more than 50 rpm. Again, the actual magnitude of the drop will vary from day to day depending on engine temperature, air temperature, etc. But in general, a large drop (without the engine roughness associated with spark plug fouling) is indicative of retarded timing, while a small drop is a sign of advanced timing.

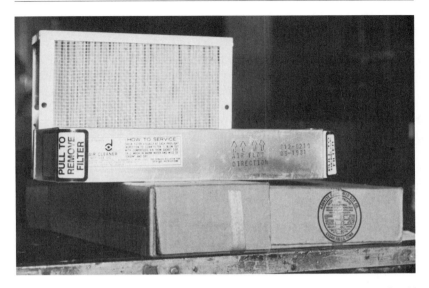

A blocked air filter can easily lead to performance degradation. Paper types should be removed no less than once every 100 hours (oftener in dusty conditions) and blown out with compressed air or washed in accordance with instructions printed on the filter.

If the rpm limits set forth above are exceeded during the mag check, pull and clean all spark plugs, then bomb-test them before putting them back in the engine. (Your FBO should have a Champion No. 2700 tester, or equivalent.) The purpose of the bomb test is to assure that plugs are not breaking down under high pressure (as exists in the combustion chamber during the compression and combustion events). Compressed air acts as a dielectric. It's important that your plugs aren't just firing under static (ambient) pressure conditions. A plug that fires normally at low pressure may (if it's defective in some way) not fire at all, or fire intermittently, at takeoff rpms and pressures. This will definitely account for a good deal of power loss.

If you can locate top dead center of piston travel on your number-one cylinder, it's a simple matter to rig a protractor and plumb line on one prop blade, then (with a hot light wired across the magneto points) check the timing of either magneto. (Have your

Bomb Test Pressures	
Plug Gap	Test Pressure
.012-in.	200 psi
.014-in.	160 psi
.016-in.	135 psi
.019-in.	115 psi
.025-in.	80 psi

mechanic show you how to find top dead center by rotating the prop both directions until the piston contacts a stop pin in the spark plug hole, noting the protractor reading at either extreme, and splitting the difference.) The timing specs for your engine will be found on the engine data plate. If you want the most power, set both mags at the advance limit. That is, if your data plate says "L and R mags, 20 deg. BTC, plus or minus 1," set the mags so the points open 21 degrees before top center of piston travel—not 19 or 20 degrees.

While you've got your spark plugs out, borrow or rent a compression tester just long enough to do a differential compression check of all cylinders (preferably with a hot engine). If any cylinder is markedly lower than the others, or if several jugs score much below 60/80, you're looking at the problem. Listen for air escaping at the breather or oil filler cap (indicating ring blowby), exhaust pipes (exhaust valve leakage), or airscoop (intake valves). Depending on how bad the leakage is, either retest in 5 or 10 hours (for jugs in the 50-to-60/80 range) or initiate a top overhaul (jugs scoring 40s-or-lower/80).

If you've done all the foregoing checks—compression is good—and the engine still is not putting out power, visually examine cam lobes and followers (and/or check valve lift at the rockers), and in solid-tappet engines (O-235, O-290) check valve clearances. Also pull all valve springs and check their compression strength per the spring test data section of the Table of Limits in your engine overhaul manual. Some years ago, Lycoming had a rash of valve-spring "loss-of-temper" episodes. The primary symptom: poor power output, especially at high rpm. While rare, the condition still gets reported.

Often when engines won't put out full power—and all the usual things have been checked—it's because muffler baffles have corroded loose and blocked the muffler outlet. This is an insidious, come-and-go type of problem. It's easy to check, however. Remove the muffler, shake it, and see if anything falls out. Or, rap on the muffler carefully with a rubber mallet and listen for rattling debris. (Obviously, the only way to make a positive check is to remove the muffler; if you can do so, do it.)

Finally, don't rule out float or diaphragm problems in carbureted and/or injected engines. (Fuel-saturated or otherwise defective floats will ride low in the carburetor bowl, giving an overrich condition.) Even the fuel itself should be considered: Many "off brands" of auto fuel contain oxygenated (alcoholic and other) blending agents, which lower the energy content of the fuel. (Amoco Premium and Shell

SU2000 are two fuels that, at this writing, do not contain oxygenates.) If you suspect fuel problems, switch vendors—and notify your local FAA district office at once.

COPING WITH HIGH OIL CONSUMPTION

Oil consumption is no longer what it once was in aviation (three *gallons*—not quarts—an hour was considered acceptable for the Wright R-1820F at high cruise), but it's still a nuisance. In an era when automobile engines seldom use a quart of oil in 50 hours (2,000 miles at 40 mph), the ten-times-higher oil usage rate of the typical airplane engine seems exorbitant indeed. We might well ask why this is so.

As it happens, car engines and airplane engines differ in many important respects (size, cooling, running clearances). The looser overall fit of top-end parts in an air-cooled engine is guaranteed to send more oil to the combustion chamber for a given cylinder wall area; and cylinder wall area is substantially greater in a 320-, 360-, or 540-cubic-inch Lycoming than in a 122-cubic-inch Toyota Celica engine.

The maximum factory specs for oil consumption for selected aircraft engines are shown in Table 1. Typical service limits are half a quart an hour for small engines, and a quart an hour for -470 and larger engines. These limits don't even come close to the Wright Cyclone's 12 quarts per hour, but oil is no longer 20 cents a quart, either. Flying an oil-burner isn't cheap anymore.

Table 1 reflects maximum-allowable burn rates (at full throttle). More typical cruise-flight usage rates are in the area of eight to twelve hours per quart for small engines (O-200, O-235, O-320, etc.) to six or eight hours per quart for larger engines (O-470, IO-520, IO-540).

The question arises: When should oil consumption be considered high enough to warrant cylinder re-

Table 1	
Manufacturers' Maximum Oil Consumption Limits for Selected Engines	
Engine	**Quarts/Hour**
O-235-C	0.5
O-320-E	0.7
O-360-A	0.8
IO-360-C	0.8
O-540-E,G,H	0.8
O-540-A,B,D	1.0
IO-540-K,L,M	1.0
TIO-540-A,C,J	1.0
TSIO-520-B,K	1.5
TSIO-520-E,WB	1.6
IO-720-A,B,C	1.7
O-470-R,S	1.8
O-470-B,G	1.9
O-470-E, J	2.2
R-1820F	12.0

moval? Opinions vary widely on this, but most knowledgeable mechanics—and factory service reps—will tell you not to get excited until oil consumption is right at the maximum book figure (a quart an hour, or whatever). Even then, it doesn't pay to get too perturbed. High oil consumption is seldom a safety-of-flight matter. The main danger is that of running out of oil on a long crosscountry leg.

"Rings will eventually carbon up and stick, maybe break," one engine overhauler remarked when asked about the consequences of longterm high-oil-usage operation. "It's not something you should let go forever, especially if you're up to a quart an hour or more."

The typical causes for high oil consumption are:

1. Poor break-in/cylinder glazing (chrome jugs especially).

.2 Ring, piston, or barrel wear; barrel scoring.

3. Ring shifting/gap lineup (should correct itself within five hours).

4. Stuck rings.

5. Valve guide wear. (If intake guides are worn, oil will drain into induction manifold after shutdown.)

6. Defective front crankshaft seal (allows ram-air pressurization of case, with breather siphoning).

7. Crankcase breather siphoning for other reasons (overfilling, blowby pressurization of case).

Continental owners who have experienced oil leakage through intake valve guides (low manifold pressure sucking oil into intake ports) can fix this problem by installing P/N 641952 valve guide seals (see Continental Service Bulletin M76-24 for details). While this fix was originally developed for the O-470, it is applicable also to E-185, E-225, IO-470, IO-520, IO-550, TSIO-520, and GTSIO-520 series engines; the same seal fits all.

Large Continental owners should also note that the factory has made four-ring pistons and a new oil-control ring available for virtually all -470 and -520 series engines. (See TCM Customer Information Bulletin CIB 87-8.)

Note that many of the above oil-consumption cause factors are interrelated. For example, stuck rings (item 4) will create enough blowby to cause crankcase pressurization and increased flow out the breather (item 7), as will gap-aligned rings (item 3). Any one item may well interact with or exacerbate any other item.

Crankcase pressurization is an insidious, widespread problem. It comes about through a variety of means (leaking front main oil seal; high piston blowby; defects in breather configuration), but it's easy to check. Any time you're curious as to whether your crankcase is pressurizing in flight, temporarily plumb a spare airspeed indicator to it and see what the pressure (IAS) indication is on the ground versus in flight. Alternatively, for ground-test purposes only, connect a manometer to the case and read crankcase pressure directly. Continental allows up to 4.0 inches H_2O static case pressure, maximum. More than this, and you've got excessive blowby.

If spark plugs are oily, compression is so-so (60/80), and consumption is high, don't look for easy cures; there's no substitute for a new-limits top overhaul. Adding STP or other oil thickeners to the sump will only carbon up the rings; and while the new multigrade oils do tend to reduce oil usage somewhat, they won't cut a quart-an-hour burn rate in half.

ENGINE VIBRATION

Vibration from the engine compartment is often hard to troubleshoot, since it is not easy to determine whether the vibration is actually due to engine roughness or some other, extraneous cause. The following checklist can be used in diagnosing "firewall-forward" vibration problems when it is not immediately known where the tremor(s) stem from.

1. Baffle to cowl clearance: Check inside surface of cowl for chafing in baffle contact areas. Trim baffles as required; repaint affected areas; reinspect after next flight.

2. Exhaust to cowl: Check tailpipe for clearance where it extends through cowl. Also, inspect stack and cowl for signs of previous chafing or contact. Enlarge cutout in cowl as required.

3. Cowl to firewall interference: On models utilizing shock-mounted cowls, positive clearance should be ensured between cowl and firewall. *Typical clearances where the cowl overlaps the fuselage run on the order of .06 to .13 inches.*

4. Induction hose clamps: Check intake hose clamp for clearance with the engine mount structure. Look for marks on engine mount. Rotate clamps as required.

5. Breather and overboard dump lines: Check all overboard dump lines from the engine for clearance with the firewall, cowl, and/or cowl flap openings. Check cowl flap in both the open and closed positions. Reposition and reclamp lines to clear.

6. Engine isolators: Check engine isolator bolt lengths. Bolts that are too long will shank out and will not apply the correct pressure to the

isolator (Lord mount). Bolts must be removed to be properly checked. Replace with next size shorter bolt if barrel nut has shanked out.

Also check Lord mounts for aging and deterioration. Replace if rubber has separated from metal pad, rubber has cracked, or the biscuit has taken a pronounced set. (Note: On engines that have not been overhauled recently, these shock mounts will sometimes be five or ten years old, and unless they've been rotated at 100-hour intervals, they will likely be in bad shape. Replacement is expensive—up to $800 per set—but could be the key to reducing engine vibration.) The first tipoff to these conditions is usually a sagging engine; check the alignment of the nose spinner with the cowl cutout.

7. Propeller: Check propeller track by setting up a reference point at the tip of one blade (hint: a properly anchored cardboard box or milk crate, marked with Magic Marker, works well) and rotating blades past this point. *Blades should not be more than 1/8" out of track.*

Also examine prop for loose or binding blades (if looseness is a problem, the tipoff will be oil or grease flung out from the base of the blades); check for loose or missing attach hardware.

If prop has been filed out recently, some change in balance may have taken place and the prop should (if vibration is noticeable) be removed for rebalancing.

8. Prop spinner: Check for visual wobble at idle. Remove spinner and check hardware (including shims) for damage or deformation. Replace defective hardware.

9. Engine controls: Curves between engine and firewall should be gentle; cables should not be stretched tight. Pull cable through firewall and reclamp as appropriate. Also, check engine controls behind engine for contact with sump or accessory case; reroute/reclamp as necessary for clearance.

10. Starter cable: Check for clearance with cowl and that a loop is provided for flexing.

11. Engine condition: Check spark plugs (for fouling, gap setting, and type), ignition harness, mag timing, magneto breaker compartment condition, engine compression, fuel injector nozzles (for obstruction), fuel pump and mixture settings, nozzle shrouds (for fuel leakage; turbocharged engines only), induction ducting and/or rubber couplings (turbo engines) for proper sealing, and the turbocharger itself (as applicable) for foreign object damage, binding, or worn bearings.

Check induction and exhaust systems particularly carefully. Replace clogged air filters. Examine throttle buttefly area for obstruction.

12. Antennas: If vibration seems to be related to airspeed rather than power setting, check antenna mounting.

13. Wheel balance and brake disc trueness: These can be sources of vibration during ground roll on some aircraft—and yes, they can mimic engine roughness.

One final piece of advice: Don't overlook the possibility that something has broken—an outright failure of an engine mount weld, an exhaust stack, muffler, etc. Such failures may be relatively rare, but are worth considering seriously if no other, obvious source of the vibration is found.

FINDING AND CORRECTING
FWF TROUBLE SIGNS

Engines require induction, oil, fuel, cooling, exhaust, and ignition systems. Any of them can leak. Leaks are generally confined, however, to deteriorated gaskets, seals, hoses, and other soft parts. Only if corrosion has set in or a baffle or flange is broken (or a case is cracked or a head blown), do hard parts leak. Consider those to be axioms and plan accordingly. Because of the related potentials for fire and fluid exhaustion problems, fuel and oil system leaks are the most critical of the collection.

Let's look at each system, one at a time:

Fuel system leaks, once we get beyond the rule tanks, are most commonly discovered at sediment bowls, due to dried out gaskets; drain sumps, due to dried out or deteriorated O-rings; electric fuel pump gaskets; loose hardware on AC fuel pumps; and to be honest, quite rarely due to deteriorated fuel lines.

Preventive maintenance measures include removing the drain sump O-rings after you have run a tank dry (do this every couple years or so), and replacing them. This is far more tidy than attempting to change an O-ring with a full tank on a 10 degree day, when leaks seem to proliferate. The cost is nominal with foresight and planning, as O-rings, unlike nearly everything else on aircraft, are not very expensive.

Moving downstream, with the engine(s) uncowled turn on the electric boost pump(s) if so equipped, and check the fuel pump housing and any lines to the carburetor or fuel injection for leaks. With somebody guarding the mixture control on fuel injected engines, have

An engine-compartment visual inspection should include a check for chafing wires or plumbing. Here, an electrical wire is seen chafing against the engine mount truss-work.

them move it into rich position while you inspect all the lines to the fuel spider and the cylinders, and the nozzles for leaks. Cracked spiders, lines or nozzles are all too common from overtightening.

With carbureted engines, remove the air filter and—with the fuel turned on and the boost pump running—check for evidence of fuel dripping from the venturi or puddling in the carb heat box. If such is the case, you have probably already discovered that you have to lean the engine quite a bit in order to keep it running, as this is symptomatic of a leaking float needle and seat, or a fuel saturated carburetor float.

While you are down there looking, take a moment and have your helper pump the throttle a couple times—the accelerator pump should squirt the better part of an ounce of fuel into the manifold each time. Don't get it in the face. The accelerator pump has a leather seal which is subject to deterioration. Generally, the only other soft parts in a carburetor are the tip of the float needle, a few gaskets, and three O-rings (two for the throttle shaft, and one for the mixture control shaft). For the most part, none of these can leak during the inspection, although the throttle shaft O-rings can cause either a lean running or rich running condition depending on which one is leaking (more of this later in an upcoming carburetor overhaul story).

Another common potential fuel leak area on infrequently used aircraft is the diaphragm on AC mechanical fuel pumps. In this type of pump, the fuel pump housing mating surfaces are held together with five or six machine screws. Every few months, particularly if you rarely fly, tighten those screws a bit—seldom will it occur to a mechanic to do so, unless you complain of erratic fuel pressure.

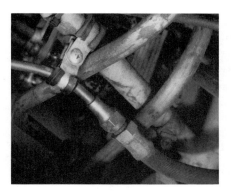

The proper way to keep plumbing from vibrating and chafing against nearby items is to use clamps. In this instance, two Adel clamps have been used to separate a fuel line from an engine mount tube. Additional clamps should be used to protect nearby breather lines.

The oil system is also subject to leaks. With Lycoming engines, the pushrods are topside of the cylinders, and their seals rarely leak, as they are as must dust covers as anything. Lycoming's tradeoff, of course, is that oil pumped to the upper cylinders through the pushrods is returned to the crankcase through aluminum external oil lines. Those lines, although they carry little pressure, are subject to vibration wear from rubbing baffle tiedowns, and could leave you with a bad oil leak.

At the line interconnect with the case, the gap is sealed with hoses secured with worm clamps.

The hardest oil leak to fix is fortunately quite uncommon; the front crankcase seal is typically a large O-ring that must be stretched over the propeller flange with a special tool. This must be done with the propeller removed, which of course adds to the expense of doing things.

Constant speed propellers can have leaks, and they mate up with the crankcase with another large O-ring. Don't confuse O-rings; we have seen a Cessna 180 lose a prop due to someone using the improper O-ring. A mechanic confused the proper O-rings for Hartzell and McCauley. Prop O-rings are installed in the grove in the propeller, and then the propeller is slipped on the engine shaft and flange. Doing it the other way risks pinching the O-ring between the mating surfaces. Props have been lost that way.

The other prospective sources of oil leaks are external oil lines to turbos, governors and oil coolers—and anything hooked onto the accessory case. We have found solid oil cooler lines to leak quite commonly at their seals, which are a bit like hollow cylinders of neoprene with grooves cut inside. As always, inspect flexible lines for hardening and external cracking, and for internal collapsing due to tight radius bends.

Induction leaks? Air box leaks can allow dust to be ingested, severely deteriorating engine life. Check gaskets and seals carefully for cracks or broken-out pieces. The other common induction leaks are in the intake manifold pipes; a leak in them normally causes a cylinder to run lean on carbureted engines, either doing damage to the valves or causing unnecessarily increased fuel consumption, as the pilot usually enriches the mixture control until the engine runs smoothly. The best evidence of such leaks is normally found by checking for fuel stains near the gaskets at the intake manifold end, and neoprene hoses at the induction spider. As with Lycoming oil return line hoses, these are secured with worm-type hose clamps. In either case, the worm clamps can and should be tightened at least annually. Replace the hoses if the worm clamps don't stay tight, as this is evidence that the neoprene has lost its resiliency.

Exhaust leaks are pretty much confined to deterioration from use, except corrosion of non-stainless steel systems. It would be improbable to find any of the copper/asbestos gasket combinations deteriorated from idleness. Notwithstanding that, white or sooty black deposits at the cylinder exhaust bosses or on the stack flanges are a matter of concern, for they are indications of a leak. Exhaust leaks here can quite rapidly erode the machined aluminum alloy cylinder bosses,

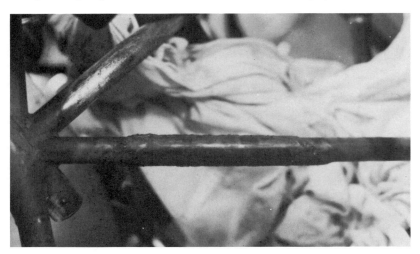

Engine mount tubes are subject to tremendous heat and will rust through if not protected. The mount in this photo has been repaired with a fishmouth sleeve splice (note weld bead). Nearby areas have been sanded in preparation for painting with high-temp enamel.

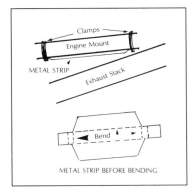

METAL STRIP BEFORE BENDING

The proper way to protect engine mounts from heat is not to wrap them with asbestos (which can trap water), but to fabricate small heat deflector shields from thin sheet steel (using tinsnips). Deflectors can be clamped directly onto mount tubes using stainless-steel clamps.

and are a potential fire hazard. When replacing an engine's exhaust gaskets, use spiral wound Blo-Proof gaskets, which are comparatively inexpensive, at a couple dollars apiece. Most people will tell you to have the exhaust stack flanges machined flat prior to reinstallation; an old mechanic's trick is to just jammer down the flange ears a bit, and the mating surfaces will match up just fine once the exhaust stud nuts are torqued down into place.

Cooling system leaks, as you might suspect, are generally confined to worn or lost baffle material, or cracks and fatigued material, or misaligned pieces. Baffle design must be an art, for if you check the average lives of engines in aircraft as diverse as Bellancas and Bonanzas, you will find that the Bellancas seem to be majored within a few hundred hours, when the identical engine will make TBO effortlessly, when installed in a different type of airplane. But that is another story.

Ignition leaks? Oil can get in the magnetos through the accessory case. But how about a bucket of electrons spilling out of the ignition harness? This occurs most commonly at high altitude with turbocharged powerplants, but can also be observed with the engine running and the cowl removed on a very dark night. If your engine seems to run rough for no other reason, give this a try, and you will believe me. Old ignition leads can break down just through old age and the effects of ozone and acid rain and all such contemporary hazards to life and property.

EXHAUST INSPECTION TIPS

Exhaust systems, to be truthful, give a lot of trouble in aviation. In high-output engine installations, turbos especially, exhaust problems are a constant threat. Something always pops, corrodes, leaks, cracks, vibrates loose, and/or disintegrates before the engine makes it to TBO. The trick is to catch it before it becomes a Real Problem costing Real Money.

If you read exhaust-system ADs (such as those pertaining to the turbocharged Cessna twins and the Piper Navajo—AD 75-23-08 and AD 79-12-03, respectively), you'll note that they tend to require only visual inspection of components—seldom dye-penetrant or other methods. This is a point worth noting. Most life-threatening exhaust-system flaws can be spotted with the naked eye.

So use your eyes. Open the cowl yourself and look the exhaust system over periodically—at least once between annuals or 100-hours (or any time the cowl is off for other reasons). Light brown, grey, or greenish exhaust stains are a tipoff to problems, naturally. But not all exhaust cracks are leakers. Sometimes it takes a very good eye indeed to spot problems.

Stains, incidentally, are often remote from the actual leak site. This is true, for example, in the case of leaks at the number-four and number-three risers on Continental O-470 engines in Skylanes. These risers are short sections held to the 1-5/2-6 'Y' risers by clamps (clamps that sometimes don't seal well). Occasionally a jet of exhaust gases will shoot past a clamp and stain an adjacent riser. Or vice versa: A bad

Welded joints should come in for extra-close scrutiny during exhaust inspections. The weld bead on this joint (in a Cessna T310 exhaust system) was found cracked on walkaround. Extensive overlap of one tube inside the other prevented a blowout. (Part was later weld-repaired and returned to service.)

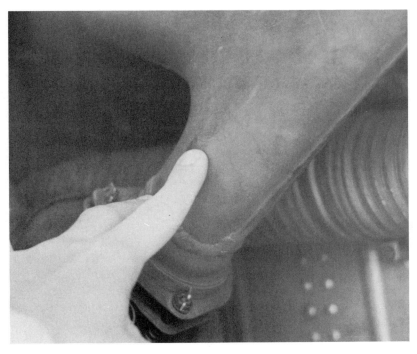

Bulges that conceal cracks can easily go unnoticed. This Bonanza cluster-riser had a one-inch hairline crack which had not yet leaked enough gas to allow staining. A sharp-eyed pilot caught it on walkaround.

exhaust gasket will let a jet of gases stain an adjacent stack, clamp, etc. Look for the true source of the stain—not just the nearest culpable component.

In dealing with clamps, it is best to remove the clamp, shift it slightly (rotate it one way or the other), and—starting with fresh nuts and bolts—reinstall it to the proper torque. Merely overtightening a leaking clamp or gasket may not get you anywhere.

Be alert for bulges in stacks or risers. Bulges usually conceal cracks (which may or may not be leaking yet). Don't throw away bulged pieces, however. A good aircraft welder can work magic on defective exhaust components, even where compound curves are present. If you don't have a good metal shop in your area, you might try Custom Aircraft Parts, 1318 Gertrude St., San Diego, CA 92110 (phone 619/276-6954). Repair of burned-out areas costs $25 to $45; new flanges are installed for $31 each; ball ends, $39.50; new flame cones installed in muffler, $71.50. (These prices were good as we went to press; naturally they may change at any time.)

When components are accessible from the inside, get out a spray can of WD40 and fog the inside of the component. The penetrant will leach to the outside of the metal wherever a crack is present, making cracks that are too small to see highly visible in a matter of two to three minutes.

To check for larger leaks (with the exhaust system installed on the airplane), obtain a vacuum cleaner that will blow clean air and plug it into the outlet of your tailpipe. (Wrap rags around it as necessary to get an air-tight seal.) Remove one spark plug from a cylinder and rotate the propeller until the exhaust valve for that cylinder is open. (Find the compression stroke the usual way, with your thumb against the hole; then continue 180 degrees.) Insert a direct-reading compression gauge in the spark-plug hole. Then power up the vacuum cleaner and adjust the leakage rate until the exhaust system is pressurized to between 10 and 15 psi.

Next, get yourself a trigger spray bottle of soap and water, and go over the entire exhaust system starting with the exhaust ports of the cylinders and ending at the muffler or lower stack. Any frothy areas, of course, indicate leakage.

Typical areas for cracks to form are as follows: Weld beads tend to absorb a lot of heat, and cracks sometimes begin forming from the outside first. These cracks often progress very slowly. Nevertheless, they should be attended to promptly. Again, this is a kind of damage that can generally be repaired by a good welder.

When exhaust gaskets (at cylinder flanges) have been found leaking, it is especially important to effect a repair quickly, rather than continue to operate the engine, since exhaust gases are hottest at this point and tend to erode the aluminum cylinder head material quickly. After removing the affected riser, examine the gasket seating surface on the cylinder. If metal is gone (leaving something less than a flat surface), the jug will almost certainly have to be removed for weld repairs—if in fact it's repairable at all. (The exhaust-pipe flange will probably be warped, but this is an easy component to fix.)

Mufflers are a discussion unto themselves, as you no doubt know. Most general aviation mufflers contain flame tubes, baffles, or other internal doodads which serve little function other than to fall out and cause trouble. When baffles or flame cones break loose, for example,

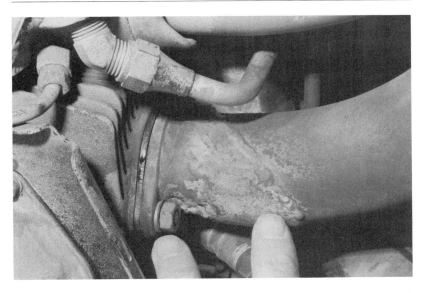

This exhaust riser has been repaired (poorly) several times in the past. Wrench access to the hold-down stud is poor, and the nut is not properly installed. (At least two threads of the stud should protrude through the end of the nut.) A blowout could easily occur here.

they can block the muffler outlet, causing exhaust back-pressure to rise to the point where the engine lugs. This can be a very frightening event, needless to say. Reason enough to take the muffler(s) off the airplane at every annual and shake them to see what falls out. (Between annuals, you can rap them with a soft mallet and listen for rattling sounds.)

FAA, by the way, approves of field installation of a muffler outlet guard to keep baffles from covering up the outlet. All you do is bend two 8-in. pieces of 3/16-in. stainless welding rod into identical U-shaped segments; braze the two Us together at the crown to form a four-legged affair; and insert the little "cage" round-end-first into the muffler outlet, welding it in place there. (We'd love to say we came up with this idea ourselves, but it's all spelled out in AC 43.13-1A.) Why FAA doesn't require muffler-makers to do this at the factory, we haven't the slightest idea.

One more tip: When you're doing your visual once-over to detect cracks, do not mark cracks' locations with grease pencil, lead pencil, or crayon. The carbon deposited by these sorts of markers will cause carbonization and localized overheating of exhaust-pipe metal, which in turn will lead to cracking. Use chalk to mark trouble spots.

Should old mufflers be repaired (remanufactured and certified airworthy), or is muffler overhauling a less-than-desirable way to go? Actually, we feel it's a very desirable way to go, provided you pick a good shop. For the ultimate in long component life, invest in Nicroflite components by Wall Colmonoy Corporation (4700 S.E. 59th St., Oklahoma City, OK 73135, phone 405/672-1361 or 365 Broadway, Montreal East, PQ, Canada H1B 5A7, phone 514/645-1683). Wall Colmonoy plasma-coats its components—both new and used—with a proprietary high-nickel coating (Nicrocoat) that literally doubles or triples the life of many exhaust components. Order through Aviall or any of the big suppliers.

For miscellanous repairs, muffler exchange, exhaust gaskets, etc., Wag-Aero's FAA repair station—Aero Fabricators, Inc.—continues to offer good selection and good service with reasonable turnaround times. (With the advent of overnight parcel service, there's no reason not to use Aero Fabricators, no matter where in the U.S. you're located.) Write Aero Fabricators at 1216 North Rd., Lyons, WI 53148 (414/763-3145) and ask for their latest exhaust parts catalog (free, at this writing). It's worth having around just to amaze your friends.

Chapter 2

CRISIS MANAGEMENT

No good statistics exist on the incidence of inflight powerplant emergencies in general aviation. Accident statistics are available, but of course these tell us nothing about actual inflight shutdown rates, because not every engine stoppage results in an accident, obviously (and not every accident gets reported, in any case).

Statistics kept by the National Transportation Safety Board show that—year after year—about one out of seven aviation accidents is caused by an engine malfunction not involving fuel starvation. In a typical year, U.S. civil aircraft rack up about 35,000,000 flight hours (or, accounting for twin-engined planes, about 40,000,000 *engine-hours*), incurring some 3,500 or so accidents, of which 500 are caused by engine problems. Thus it's possible to estimate that there is one

NTSB-investigated engine malfunction every 80,000 engine-operating hours (approximately)—or, since the average engine goes 2,000 hours between overhauls, there's one engine-failure accident every 40 TBO runs. Many, if not most, engine stoppages are related to poor maintenance, however. If failures due to inadequate upkeep are removed from the total, the picture brightens considerably. (Accidents categorized by NTSB as due to "powerplant failure for undetermined reasons" account for only 250 mishaps per year, of which less than 10 percent are fatal.)

Your chances of having an enroute power interruption are small. But if you fly long enough, you're bound to experience *some* mechanical difficulties while airborne. The question is: Will you know how to cope?

Remember that with very few exceptions, a light plane needs only 25 percent power, roughly, to sustain flight (less in ground effect). The goal, when managing any type of engine problem, is always the successful—preferably the on-airport—termination of the flight. If you can get the engine to put out *some* power, chances are good you can make it to the nearest airport. (Even without power, the odds of a survivable off-airport touchdown are good—*if you continue to fly the airplane.*)

No matter what the problem, always remember:

1. Fly the airplane. (Turn on the autopilot if you intend to devote full attention to solving the engine problem, but *do not engage the altitude-hold feature.* Select *attitude* hold—or simply trim the plane for minimum-descent speed.)

2. Reduce power. In almost any engine-malfunction emergency, the thermal and mechanical loadings on the engine can be reduced (and the likelihood of continued safe operation increased) by simply throttling back.

3. Don't continue flying with a sick engine. After a powerplant problem has been uncovered, land *as soon as practicable.*

Sudden engine roughness is arguably the most common, and hardest to troubleshoot, FWF (firewall-forward) complaint. One person's "loud noise" is another person's "resonant vibration," and it is often difficult to tell prop or engine-mount problems apart from bonafide ignition or combustion aberrations. Nevertheless, certain guidelines apply:

First, if you're flying in humid conditions (i.e., visibility less than ten miles) and you have a carbureted engine, *turn on the carburetor heat.* (Be ready for a large, temporary power loss if carb ice slushes off and enters the engine.)

Secondly, observe the engine compartment for obvious signs of damage (con rods sticking through the cowling, etc.), oil or fuel leaks, smoke or flame, or anything unusual. If anything odd is evident, the most appropriate action will usually be to reduce power. (It goes without saying that if you're on fire, you should engage the extinguisher system and/or turn off the fuel at the fuel selector.)

Thirdly, *consult the engine instruments.* If abnormal EGT, CHT, oil temperature, oil pressure, tach, or manifold pressure indications appear, take appropriate action(s) as outlined below. (If fuel flow is fluctuating, engage the auxiliary fuel pump. *Fuel-flow fluctuations are almost always caused by vapor bubbles in the lines.*)

Fourth, attempt to *reset the power controls* so as to "smooth out" the engine. After throttling back and experimenting with prop rpm, *reset the mixture.* Keep all adjustments gradual, however. Do *not* automatically shove the mixture control into the "full rich" position (see below). It's possible, especially in a turbocharged aircraft—or a plane with an especially powerful electric fuel pump—for the roughness to be the result of an already overrich mixture. Going to full-rich may well make the engine quit cold.

After you've adjusted the power knobs (and assuming the roughness has not totally gone away), check out the ignition system. Turn each magneto off one at a time to check for a defective harness or mag. (Do this only after reducing power as described above.) If the engine smooths out after one magneto has been shut off, *leave the bad mag off* and continue to the nearest maintenance base. There's nothing wrong with flying on one magneto in a situation such as this. (That's what you have two of them for.) The only problem is that in initially determining which—if any—of your mags is bad, you may well kill the engine when and if (in the process of troubleshooting) the faulty mag is selected. In the event you select one or the other mag, and the engine quits, *momentarily reduce throttle and move the mixture to idle cutoff before turning the ignition back on.* (This will prevent a potentially damaging backfire.) Once the "good" mag has been found, of course, you can readjust throttle, rpm, and mixture as necessary to continue the flight.

If the engine has sustained physical damage of a kind that prevents it from running smoothly, there may be little or nothing you can do from the cockpit to prevent it from shaking. This is true, for example, of valve-sticking episodes in which pushrods take a permanent bend. (One also hears of valve lifters occasionally collapsing in mid-flight, producing a peculiar roughness that may or may not disappear later. This can be hard to troubleshoot.)

In any case, bear in mind the following bit of advice, given in the Continental TSIO-360-F *Operator's Manual* (p. 19): "WARNING: Severe roughness may be sufficient to cause propeller separation. Do not continue to operate a rough engine unless there is no other alternative."

High-Altitude Roughness

Roughness at (or going to) oxygen altitudes is a tipoff to ignition problems. The reason is simple. Magnetos do not generate a fixed voltage, but produce (by flyback effect) whatever output is, in effect, needed to jump the gap at the spark plug electrodes under any given set of conditions. Since air is electrically insulating, it takes more voltage to fire a spark plug under high-pressure conditions than low-pressure conditions. Conversely, it takes less voltage to spark a gap at altitude (in a partial vacuum) than under standard sea-level conditions. The net effect is that at some sufficiently high altitude—perhaps as low as 12,000 feet, perhaps 20,000 feet or more (it depends on the electrode gap and many other factors)—a high-tension magneto will "spark out" internally rather than fire the spark plug. Electricity always takes the path of least resistance. Often that path is inside the magneto itself, at high altitude.

If misfiring is encountered at altitude, *reduce manifold pressure and increase rpm.* Also, *descend to a lower altitude.* Continuing to fly with a misfiring engine is not a good idea, even if the misfire is only occasional, as severe engine damage can occur.

Cleaning and gapping your spark plugs will help forestall high-altitude misfire (as will replacing any "leaky" ignition wires), but the ultimate answer to the problem is magneto pressurization. (Magnetos pressurized with turbo bleed air are standard equipment on post-1981 Cessna T210, P210, and T303 aircraft as well as the Mooney 231, Piper's Navajo Chieftain and Malibu, Turboplus-modified Turbo Arrows and Senecas, and RAM-modified Cessna 340 and 414 aircraft.)

Aside from magneto arcing, the other major cause of engine roughness at high altitude is fuel-flow fluctuation due to vapor formation in fuel lines. (Lines can easily become heat-soaked after a long climb to altitude). If fuel-flow is fluctuating, energize the boost pump(s). Some

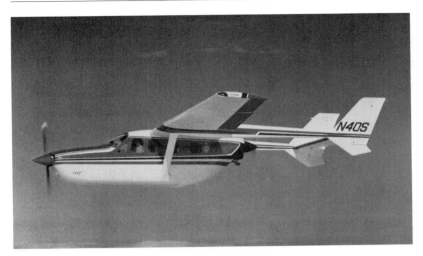

Magneto misfire is much more likely in a high-flying aircraft, such as the Cessna Pressurized Skymaster. Reduced ambient air pressure inside the magneto makes for easier ionization; distributor crossfire is a very real hazard, unless pressurized magnetos are installed.

operating handbooks (such as those for the Cessna twins) advise leaving auxiliary fuel pumps on, prophylactically, at altitudes above 12,000 feet, until engine temperatures stabilize in level cruise.

The Universal Checklist

Episodes of sudden, major power loss (with no warning symptoms) are rare in aviation, thankfully. Most such problems stem from misfueling, fuel exhaustion, or failure to remove water from sumps (occasionally vapor lock during a hot-day flight using substandard fuel). We will confine our discussion here to enroute power interruptions, for which there is a sort of universal checklist (for *normally aspirated engines only*):

1. Boost pump—ON (unless specified otherwise in the owner's manual).

2. Fuel selector—SWITCH TANKS. (If you are already on the fullest tank, consider switching to another tank anyway. The first tank may not be venting properly, or it may contain condensation, bad fuel, etc.)

3. Mixture—RICH.

4. Alternate air—ON. (Turn OFF again if no improvement is noted.)

5. Magnetos—verify BOTH. (Try each mag independently if there is time.)

6. Primer—SECURED (in and locked).

7. Engine instruments—OBSERVE for indications of trouble. (If abnormal indications are found, refer to the appropriate sections further below.)

On an airplane equipped with a constant-speed prop, select low pitch. The high rpm will, among other things, enable the magnetos to deliver a more energetic spark to the spark plugs.

Always remember that if fuel, air, and spark are present, combustion *has to occur*. The object of any "inflight power loss" checklist is to restore fuel, air, and spark to the engine, in quantities that will support combustion. If the checklist procedures fail to restore power, it may mean the engine has sustained physical damage of a type that precludes further operation. (For example, all oil may have

In a turbocharged aircraft (such as the Piper Seneca II), any extended period of roughness or misfire at high altitude may well cause turbocharger rundown (and further power loss) due to the reduced exhaust flow through the turbo. The engine manufacturer's operating handbook procedure should be followed exactly. Merely going to full-rich mixture at the first sign of trouble may cause a "rich-out."

been lost overboard, or the oil pump may have failed, causing bearing failure.)

The above checklist is not to be used if it contradicts any advice given in the aircraft owner's manual. (Some manuals advise turning the boost pump off immediately, for example, if turning it on briefly doesn't make the engine run better.) Also, as mentioned above, this checklist is for normally aspirated engines only; turbocharged engines are subject to different procedures, outlined further below.

Turbocharger Run-Down

In a turbocharged engine operating at high altitude (above 12,000 feet), a transient interruption in fuel flow that might be acceptable in some other kinds of engines—such as might happen when running a fuel tank dry—can cause engine failure due to turbocharger spooldown. (The power loss may or may not be complete, and may or may not be accompanied by surging of rpm, fuel flow, and/or manifold pressure.) In high-altitude operation, a small turbo such as an AiResearch T04 or Rajay 325E reaches turbine speeds of up to 100,000 rpm. Any interruption of exhaust flow to the turbine will cause it to slow down immediately. At the same time, compressor output will fall and a transient overrich mixture condition will develop. If fuel flow to the engine is then increased (by going to full rich, activating the boost pump, or switching from an empty to a full tank), the engine may quit.

If your plane is turbocharged, follow the air-restart procedures in your owner's manual. If you do *not* have an air-restart checklist, do the following:

1. Mixture—IDLE CUTOFF.

2. Fuel selector—FULL TANK, or in a position that will permit the use of the electric boost pump.

3. Boost pump—ON (low position, if there is both a low and a high setting).

4. Throttle—OPEN to normal cruise position.

5. Propeller—HIGH RPM (cruise rpm or higher).

6. Mixture—ENRICH SLOWLY from idle cutoff. When engine restarts (indicated by a surge of power), continue to monitor fuel flow and make mixture adjustments as the turbocharger slowly comes up to full speed. Operate at 18 inches MP at first, then readjust power levers and boost pump(s) as required for cruise.

If this procedure fails to result in a quick restart, it may be because you are at too high an altitude for normally aspirated combustion to occur. (Remember, above 12,000 feet the air is thin and you will get no more than a fraction of sea-level horsepower if the engine does restart. Also, you may be working against a closed wastegate, which creates significant exhaust back-pressure.) Your chances of a successful "relight" increase substantially at lower altitudes.

At high altitudes, low OAT and high IAS combine to produce impressive wind-chill factors. The result may be a hard-to-restart engine. As Continental explains in its TSIO-360-F *Operator's Manual,* "A few minutes' exposure to temperatures and airspeed at flight altitudes can have the same effect on an inoperative engine as hours of cold-soak in sub-Arctic conditions. If the engine must be restarted, consideration should be given to descending to warmer air (first)."

Engine Fire

Inflight engine fires come about, typically, through breakage of old hoses and fittings, failure of exhaust components, external fuel leakage from fuel injectors, arcing at chafed wires, and piston holing (which allows combustion gases to enter the crankcase directly, setting the oil on fire). Although no good statistics exist, fires are probably more prevalent in turbocharged-engine installations than unturbocharged systems; more prevalent in twins (with their tightly packed cowlings) than in singles; and perhaps more common in older planes than in newer ones. Good maintenance will go a long way toward preventing inflight fires.

It's a good idea to turn the master switch off (to eliminate any electricity that may be causing arcing) as soon as possible after detecting smoke or flames. If you have a battery-powered portable comm radio, use it (and your ELT) to signal an emergency.

Pulling the mixture to idle cutoff will cut off fuel at the flow divider or carburetor, but that may well be downstream of the fire's point of origin. To eliminate the fuel flow *upstream* of the origin, *turn the fuel selector off.* (This is one of very few good times to turn a fuel selector off.) After that, you can pull the mixture back all the way—if in fact it will move at all (chances are, it's melted somewhere ahead of the firewall)—and turn the boost pump off (if it was on). Also secure the primer.

Cessna makes the recommendation in its Turbo 182 Owner's Manual that if, after going through the inflight fire checklist (which includes retrimming the aircraft for 100 knots) the fire has not gone out, the pilot ought to "increase glide speed to find an airspeed which will provide an incombustible mixture." In other words, blow out the fire by diving. (Another good reason to select a high glide speed: it gets you on the ground quicker.)

Your inflight-engine-fire checklist ought to look something like this:

1. Master switch—OFF as soon as possible. (Call Mayday first, if you are going to.)

2. Fuel selector—OFF as soon as possible. (Do this before fooling with mixture or boost pump, etc.)

3. Mixture—IDLE CUTOFF (if it hasn't melted already).

4. Boost pump—OFF.

5. Primer—SECURED.

6. Cabin heat—OFF (to prevent smoke entry into cockpit).

7. Airspeed—ADJUST to minimize time in the air, and to find an airspeed that will provide an incombustible (or at least less combustible) mixture.

8. Cowl flaps—ADJUST to minimize flames/smoke.

9. Stick & rudder—SIDESLIP to keep flames away from cabin.

10. Gear & flaps—LOWER MANUALLY if fire has not gone out, prior to touchdown (at pilot's discretion).

11. Emergency exit—OPEN just before touchdown. (Many times, doors and emergency exits get jammed shut on a hard landing as the fuselage deforms under load. Pop the latch before you hit, so you can get out.)

If the fire self-extinguishes before touchdown, you might be tempted to turn the master switch back on (to lower the gear, for example). It's probably a bad idea, especially if one or more circuit breakers has popped. Plan on using the emergency gear system.

It should be mentioned that Enk Total Flood (and factory-installed) nacelle fire detection and extinguishing systems require regular maintenance and in many cases have life-limited components. Do not neglect these components at annual-inspection time. There's nothing worse than carrying around a bulky, costly fire extinguishing system, only to find that it doesn't work when it is really needed.

Low Oil Pressure

Pressure oil lubrication is what keeps a reciprocating engine reciprocating. (It's also, in large part, what keeps an air-cooled engine cool.)

Total loss of oil pressure, whether because of oil-pump failure, oil starvation, or for other reasons, can have dramatic consequences. At some point, bearings seize and the prop simply stops cold. If you're *really* unlucky, a connecting rod comes through the windshield and causes dental problems.

This isn't to say, of course, that an engine won't continue operating with oil pressure just below the green arc. Pilots tend to underestimate an aircraft engine's ability to run with low oil pressure *at low power settings*. High crankshaft speeds, high temperatures, and high brake mean effective pressures put a high demand on lubricating oils. Reduce the demands, and the oil's "operating envelope" is expanded. As long as temperatures and power settings (and rpm) are not high, many engines will drone along without damage at oil pressures as low as 10 or 20 psi. Most engines will idle for at least short periods, without damage to bearings or lifters, at pressures less than 10 psi. (A lot depends on where and how you measure the pressure, however, and the grade/quality of oil.) A full-power go-around requires significant oil pressure, on the other hand (as do turbo bearings and wastegate actuators).

The first thing to do when low or fluctuating oil pressure is noted (fluctuation usually signalling oil-pump cavitation or imminent oil exhaustion) is *reduce power*.

The second thing to do after noting a low oil-pressure indication is look at the oil-temperature gauge. When oil flow through the engine galleries slows down (as it inevitably must when pressure falls off), oil temperature rises. (The rise in temperature thins the oil and reduces pressure even further.) If high oil temp is noted, open the cowl flaps and trim for a higher airspeed. (Since you've already reduced power, this means descending.)

If oil temperature is *not* high and you have a low pressure indication, suspect a bad gauge rather than a bonafide oil-pressure problem. Of course, oil pooling on the cabin floor from a source behind the panel means you have a bad connection at the gauge. Not to worry, however. The pressure gauge plumbing contains a restrictor orifice designed to prevent severe, rapid loss of oil from the sump in case of a plumbing failure; hence, you are in no immediate danger if the problem is leaky plumbing. (You should land immediately and have the problem checked out, nevertheless.)

Low oil pressure doesn't have to mean mechanical problems: It often happens that a tiny bit of carbon or sludge will block the orifice in the gauge plumbing, causing the cockpit instrument to indicate erratically. Problems of this sort are by no means uncommon. The tipoff is always low pressure in conjunction with normal oil temperature indications (and normal engine behavior). Continued flight is permissible, provided gauges are monitored closely for changes.

When oil pressure falls into the "limbo zone" just below the bottom of the green (but above, say, 25 psi), with oil temperatures high but not at redline, it is usually advisable to continue the flight to the nearest convenient maintenance base. Any time oil pressure falls into a red or yellow arc, however (or below 20 psi, in general)—accompanied by a sharp rise in oil temperature—there is some danger of engine failure, and the pilot should plan accordingly. If pressure is extremely low (and oil temperature high), a precautionary landing should be made *asap*—off-airport, if necessary.

High Cylinder Head Temp

When the CHT gauge reads high, it's often difficult to know whether you have an overtemp merely in one cylinder (i.e., the one to which the sensing probe is attached) or all cylinders. (EGT doesn't give a reliable crosscheck, since CHT can increase as EGT goes down, and vice versa.)

A CHT in the high 400s (Fahrenheit) is usually a reliable tipoff to trouble. CHT redlines are variously set at 460 and 500 degrees. Anything above 435 can be considered detrimental to the longterm health of the cylinder head, and anything approaching redline is cause for genuine concern. The answer is to reduce power, enrich mixture (to the extent that it is possible to do so without causing engine roughness), open any cowl flaps, and—if the aircraft is at high altitude (above 12,000 feet)—try a lower cruise altitude. If practical, the airplane should also be trimmed nose-down for a higher airspeed.

Of course, reducing power in level flight reduces airspeed, too, which would seem to be a poor thing to do in the event of CHT overtemping. In fact, though, an airplane's engine is much better at producing heat than propulsive power (airspeed). It takes a very large increase in power to get a relatively small increase in airspeed; and the reverse is also true. By throttling back, you cut heat production dramatically, at the expense of very little loss in cooling airflow.

Going to a lower altitude may not seem to make much sense (after all, the air is much cooler at high altitude, isn't it?), but the fact is that air density—which is a controlling variable for cooling—falls off so rapidly at higher altitudes (along with indicated airspeed and cooling drag) that the low outside air temperature doesn't compensate. Cooling is worse up high than down low. So when overtemping is a problem, *go lower* (to where indicated airspeeds are higher).

An abnormally high CHT indication can often be brought down to acceptable levels by a combination of mixture enrichment, opening cowl flaps, and/or reducing power or altitude. When it can't, you're more than likely looking at one or more of the following:

—a partially clogged injector nozzle (which will cause a lean-out in just one cylinder);

—deteriorated engine cooling baffles;

—an induction air leak;

—advanced mag timing;

—fuel pump or injector system or carburetor not set up within specified fuel-flow limits;

—preignition;

—detonation.

Bad fuel will cause detonation, as will aggressive leaning at high power settings (or even at moderate power settings, at high altitude, in some turbocharged engines), or for that matter improperly advanced timing. If you have just had your magnetos worked on, suspect the latter. Regardless of the cause, if detonation is suspected, reduce power and *enrichen the mixture*.

High Oil Temperature

High oil temp and low oil pressure go hand in hand. Therefore crosscheck the two gauges, and before believing either one, see if it agrees with the other. Prolonged high oil temperature, not accompanied by a significant dip in oil pressure, may be indicative of nothing more than a faulty capillary or thermocouple, which is quite common.

The circumstances under which high oil temperature manifests itself can be important in diagnosing the source of the problem. For example, many engines have a so-called "vernatherm valve" at the oil cooler which acts thermostatically to shunt oil away from the cooler any time the temperature demands on the oil are not large. Hangups in this valve are common. Oil temp typically builds and builds after takeoff, reaching near-redline levels (where it may stay for quite some time) before—suddenly and for no apparent reason—plunging to the low green. This is the tipoff to a sticky vernatherm. Any time wildly fluctuating oil temperature is noted, the thermostatic bypass valve should be removed and inspected. In some cases, it's advisable to put a thicker or thinner gasket under the vernatherm valve, to increase or decrease the distance the valve has to move (thereby altering its sensitivity).

Oil coolers occasionally become clogged with sludge, cooling fins become bent, etc., and depending on the design and location, coolers also can become vapor-locked (with air bubbles trapped in the high spots in the system). Check engine cooling baffles and general cowling condition, to make sure the oil cooler is getting the proper amount of blast air. (Remove the remains of birds' nests, etc.) If after checking all the "easy" things you *still* haven't pinpointed the cause of chronic high oil temperature, pull the accessory case cover and check the oil pump. Also check the suction screen for blockage.

The grade of oil used—and the amount—will have an effect on oil temp, naturally, as will OAT. While most aircraft engines can be safely operated in normal flight attitudes with as little as two quarts of oil in the sump, it is desirable from a cooling standpoint never to dip below the minimum level specified in the airplane owner's manual (usually six quarts).

SUDDEN STOPPAGE

What do you do when your engine has been involved in propeller tip loss, sudden stoppage due to a gear malfunction, or other, similar trauma? Do you incur the expense of tearing the engine down for

Sudden stoppage needn't automatically mean an engine teardown. In all cases, however, a check should be made of crankshaft runout (at the prop flange). If runout exceeds the manufacturer's recommendation, a teardown is unavoidable. In some cases, crankshafts may be "bent back" and reused. Large Continental cranks will have to undergo ultrasonic testing.

inspection—even though the engine looks and sounds normal? Do you dare continue the engine in service without *any* inspection? If not, what kinds of inspections should be undertaken?

The engine manufacturers, naturally, have their own answers to these questions…carefully worded answers, designed more to protect the companies' legal interests than to shed light on the complexities of sudden-stop damage and inspections.

Briefly, the engine manufacturers' positions can be summed up as follows:

Continental insists that complete engine disassembly (with magnetic-particle inspection of the crankshaft, gears, and connecting rods, and Zyglo inspection of the crankcase) is "the only sure method" of ascertaining the extent of damage following sudden engine stoppage. Continental maintains that it is useless to try to predict the extent of possible internal damage based on the circumstances surrounding the incident (i.e., engine rpm, aircraft forward speed, type of material impacting the prop, and so on). The company position is spelled out in Service Bulletin No. M71-5.

Lycoming's policy (as stated in Service Letter L163B) is that in the case of sudden engine stoppage—or the loss of a blade tip or an entire propeller—the "safest procedure is to remove and disassemble the engine and completely inspect the reciprocating parts." (We believe that Lycoming means to say "all moving parts" rather than merely "reciprocating parts." By definition, an engine's reciprocating parts are those that move back and forth—the pistons, valves, etc.—and do not include the crankshaft, camshaft, or oil-pump gears.)

Unlike the folks at Continental, Lycoming *will* go so far as to say that "the severity of the damage to the propeller and suddenness of the stoppage must be two factors on which to base judgment as to whether inspection of the engine is required. For example, it is generally accepted that minor propeller damage will not cause hidden internal damage and the engine can be continued in service with reasonable assurance of trouble-free operation."

Interestingly, in an earlier (no longer active) version of Lycoming Service Letter L163, the phrase "minor propeller damage" is written "minor propeller damage of *less than the four inches at the blade tip.*"

Neither Lycoming Service Letter L163B nor Continental Service Bulletin M71-5 contains a great deal of specific advice regarding the inspection or return to service of engines involved in prop strikes. Based on our own experience in this area, we would like to offer the following comments and observations concerning the return to service of "traumatized" engines:

[1] If the engine is more than 60% of the way to attainment of its full TBO, or if the engine was developing considerable power when stoppage occurred, consider a premature major overhaul. You were going to overhaul it in a few hundred hours anyway.

[2] If damage to the airframe is expected to take months to repair (and it probably will, given the difficulty in obtaining parts these days), have the engine pickled for long-term storage. If you fail to do this—and you elect to return the engine to service *sans* overhaul—internal corrosion will take place . . . *ensuring* the need for a premature overhaul.

[3] Consult a factory representative, or a knowledgeable mechanic, to determine whether your engine has tuned crankshaft counterweights, and—if it does—to determine whether the circumstances surrounding your engine's stoppage are likely to have caused *detuning* of the counterweights. Do not attempt to operate the engine until this information has been obtained.

[4] Determining whether damage has occurred to the crankshaft is your main concern following any instance of sudden engine stoppage. Therefore, before returning a traumatized engine to service (without a teardown inspection), have your mechanic check the crankshaft for runout, as well as for cracks on the back side of the propeller flange (at the radius to the shaft). These checks can be made on the aircraft, with the engine fully assembled. (Naturally, if the crankshaft exceeds runout limits, a complete teardown is required.)

If all signs are positive and a decision to return the engine to service (sans teardown) is reached, it is highly advisable that the pilot keep a close watch on oil pressure indications *now and for the TBO life of the engine*. Aside from crankshaft damage, your other main worry following an instance of sudden engine stoppage is *cracking of the crankcase*. Not just external cracking, but fracturing of the bearing webs and/or oil passages. The latter—if it has occurred—may well grow worse with time, leading to ever-lower oil pressure indications in the cockpit. It pays to be alert to this.

Good operating practice (and common sense) dictates that a returned-to-service engine be inspected frequently. Oil screens (and/or filter elements) should be inspected for metal within the first 10 hours of post-trauma operation, and every 25 hours thereafter. Also, fine-tooth-comb inspection of the crankcase exterior for cracks should be made a part of every 100-hour inspection.

Finally, any traumatized engine that has been returned to service without being torn down should be put on a strict once-every-50-hours oil analysis (if it's not already on such a schedule), to detect rapid bearing wear resulting from exessive crankshaft deformation.

These observations are, of course, meant to supplement—not re-place—the recommendations given in Lycoming Service Letter L163B and Continental Service Bulletin M71-5. We present these observations for educational purposes only. Any decision to continue a traumatized engine in service *without* benenfit of a complete tear-down inspection must be the responsibility of the aircraft owner/operator, in accordance with FAR 91.163(a).

OIL-LEAK TROUBLESHOOTING AND CORRECTION

Have you ever noticed the way some engines—older ones espe-cially—seem to ooze oil from every flange, bolt, and parting line? The older an engine gets, it seems, the more it tends to want to seep oil and/or burn it. After a while, it can be difficult to tell how much of an engine's total oil consumption is due to combusion, how much due to breather loss, and how much due to seepage or leakage. (Also, after a while, an engine compartment can get so grimy that tracing a leak to its origin can be anything but simple.)

Slow seepage of oil (from governors, rocker box covers, etc.) doesn't necessarily spell trouble, of course. But it's always worth finding out where a leak is coming from—and stopping it, if possible. The innocu-ous drip-drop of oil from the underside of the cylinder head may indicate nothing more serious than a leaky pushrod housing seal (which is easily dealt with—see below). On the other hand, it may be the telltale first sign of a cracked cylinder head casting (a problem with TSIO-360 Continentals, for example). In either case, you've got a potential safety hazard (all you need is for a bit of runoff to drip onto an exhaust riser, and you've got an inflight fire), and appropriate countermeasures are called for.

Diagnosis

Tracing an oil isn't always easy, but the first step is always the same: Clean the engine compartment. (This is something that, according to

Appendix D of FAR Part 43, mechanics are supposed to do during each annual or 100-hour inspection, but may shops ignore this rule.) Combine this step with your next oil/filter change, and you'll kill two birds with one flint.

A solvent wash (as opposed to a soap wash) is usually best. Start by covering all electrical accessories—mags, starter, alternator, vibrator, voltage regulator—with Saran wrap and tape, and also cover up the vacuum pump if it's a dry type. Many magnetos' internal parts are waxed to prevent arc-over, and unless vent holes are covered during washing, the wax could be dissolved. Likewise, dry pumps' carbon innards are (according to Airborne) damaged by exposure to Stoddard solvent. Cover up not only the intake/exhaust tube(s), but the drive pad area (the pump drive is usually open to the atmosphere).

Next, obtain a two-gallon garden sprayer, fill it with a high-flash-point petroleum-spirits solvent (Stoddard or Varsol), and spray the cold or warm—never hot—engine top and bottom. (Also, clean the inside of the top cowl—you'll want to note oil spray patterns later.) Caked-on grime can be dislodged with a bristle brush (but not a wire brush). Avoid inundating air filters or vacuum relief valves.

Incidentally, automotive engine cleaners (Gunk aerosol or equivalent) are fine to use on airplane engines. But don't under any circumstances use Easy-Off Oven Cleaner (or any other caustic household product) on your Lycoming or Continental. Easy-Off contains sodium hydroxide (lye), which will permeate the pore structure of aluminum castings and cause permanent damage.

Brief exposure of Plexiglas to Stoddard solvent or Varsol is not harmful, as long as it is wiped (or water-rinsed) away eventually.

After allowing the solvent to act for ten minutes or so, hose the engine down with water (preferably warm water). Allow the engine to air-dry, and remove all protective plastic covers.

Finally, take a moment to relubricate governor and throttle linkages, alternate air hinges, cowl flap hinges, etc. with clean, lightweight oil. (Hint: First drive out residual water with a blast of WD-40, which contains water displacement agents. Water displacement . . . WD . . . get it?)

Initial Checkpoints

After running the engine, you're now in a position to trace leaks or drips with a minimum of hassle. Some typical checkpoints include the prop governor (base and control end), accessory pads, crankcase parting line, cylinder bases, pushrod housings, rocker cover gaskets, oil filler necks, sump quick-drains, breather tubes, oil separator connections, and induction system drains. (Yes, induction system drains. Engines with worn intake-valve guides often suck enough oil through the guides—during low-manifold-pressure operation—to result in a constant slow flow of oil from intake ports to induction-system low point.)

Incidentally, leakage at the crankcase spine is not unheard-of in new or just-overhauled engines, particularly if (as is often in the situation in cheap field overhauls) the case halves were not checked for true (and/or re-line-bored) before assembly. Of course, silk thread is traditionally placed between the case halves—even in a field overhaul—to prevent such leakage (although in reality, this has now largely been supplanted by the use of RTV silicone rubber), but there is a fair amount of technique involved in laying silk thread—and there is a fair amount of crankcase warpage in aircraft engines. (Even those that never leaked *before* can start leaking after overhaul, since—once a case is dissassembled—internal stresses let the metal move.) Unless oil leakage is severe, "wet spine syndrome" can generally be ignored. It'll cure itself in 200-300 hours, as normal gum deposits form inside the engine.

Bonafide crankcase *cracks* are another story. As a rule, cracks originating from the lower portion (bottom two thirds of circumference) of a cylinder base pad are bad news and mean grounding the airplane. Ditto for cracks longer than two inches in length (any location), or any crack that actually *leaks* (not seeps) oil in any significant quantities. Many crankcase cracks are safely flyable, however, and some can be stop-drilled and filled with epoxy. (See AD 77-13-22.) For further information on what constitutes a flyable vs. an unflyable case crack, see Teledyne Continental Service Bulletin M83-10, Revision 1 (September 6, 1983), or seek the counsel of the nearest available factory service rep.

Incidentally, owners of Lycoming IO-540-K engines (Bellanca Vikings, Piper/Smith Aerostars, Piper Saratogas, Cherokee Sixes, Braves) should pay close attention to the crankcase areas adjacent the No. 1 cylinder base pad, at the 1/2-inch hold-down stud. This area has been known to crack at low time.

Although not part of the engine per se, the propeller (if it's constant-speed) can leak engine oil. Here, let common sense be your guide. If the oil spray is light and occasional (i.e., happens only once every few weeks, on initial startup after a period of inactivity), just continue to fly and keep an eye on it. If, on the other hand, the spray is heavy and constant (getting thicker all the time), heed the handwriting on the plasterboard. Schedule a prop teardown.

Don't mistake thrown hub grease or engine front-seal overspray for prop oil, however; examine the spray pattern carefully to determine the most likely origin. (Spray patterns inside the cowling can be helpful here.)

And if oil is coming out your (turbo'd) airplane's exhaust pipe, don't be quick to blame the turbocharger. "Most of the turbochargers that come in here for oil leakage," explains a spokesman for a large west-coast turbo overhaul shop, "aren't leaking oil at all. It's almost always a check-valve or installation problem."

Gasket Leaks

Aircraft engines have four or six individual head gaskets, and a corresponding number of chances for mischief. Repeated reuse of old gaskets is usually the culprit in any oil-leakage episode, whether it involves gaskets for rocker covers or for prop governors or other accessories. If a rocker box is dripping oil (and there's no obvious sign of damage—such as a shifted rocker-shaft wearing a hole in the rocker cover, which is not uncommon in small Lycomings), remove the valve cover and replace the gasket yourself. Gaskets are inexpensive and obtainable at virtually any FBO. (You can also order them by mail from Precision Air Parts, Inc., P.O. Box 336, Wetumpka, AL 36092, phone 205/285-6213. Complete single-cylinder gasket sets for most Lycoming and Continental engines run $5.98 to $9.00, including intake and exhaust gaskets—and cylinder-base O-rings—in addition to the valve-cover gasket itself.)

After unscrewing all valve-cover fillister screws (keep them in an FAA-approved Dixie cup until needed), gently pry away the valve cover while holding a drip try under it to catch the tablespoon or so of oil that's usually trapped inside the rocker compartment. You may need a razor blade or other scraper to remove all of the old gasket. (Be careful not to gouge the metal; that may be why there's a leak there in the first place.) Stop and take a moment to inspect the rocker compartment. The rocker-boss ears should show no evidence of cracking, everything should look well-lubricated, and—while some hard-carbon "coffee ground" type deposits are normal—there should be no heavy deposit buildup.

Before installing any new gasket, you should check to be sure the mating suface is clean and free of gouges, nicks, dents, cracks, etc. (Call in a mechanic if you find anything unusual.) Wet the new gasket with oil—as you would an oil-filter gasket—before installing it. Put the rocker cover back on, and install the hold-down screws as before, with lockwashers as appropriate.

Pushrod Seals

In Continental engines, which have pushrods running below the cylinders, oil leakage at pushrod shroud tube seals can be a problem. (Rocker box oil is returned to the crankcase by gravity, via these shroud tubes.) In Lycoming engines—which have pushrods *above* the cylinders—such oil leakage is much rarer. (Return oil finds its way to the sump via individual rocker-box drain tubes at the bottoms of the heads.) Hence, we'll concentrate on dealing with leaky Continental pushrod seals—although if you can follow the procedures outlined below, you shouldn't have any trouble replacing Lycoming seals.

Step one in replacing pushrod seals is to remove the valve cover (see section immediately above). With the rocker compartment exposed, you can then proceed to "unload" the pushrods by turning the propeller by hand until both valves close (watch the rocker action). For safety's sake, be sure the switch is off, the mixture is in idle cutoff, and the engine is cold before hand-turning the prop.

When both valves are 100-percent closed, and *only* when they're closed, you can go ahead and slide the rocker shaft(s) sideways, in order to liberate the rockers and expose the pushrods themselves. Clip any safety-wire that may be present on the rocker shaft retainer bolts (see O-470 head photo, accompanying). Remove each bolt, tap the rocker shafts sideways just enough to free the rockers (you don't actually want to remove the shafts themselves), and lift out each rocker. Be sure to note the number and position of any thrust washers that may be present on either side of either rocker. Also, as a general rule, you don't want to mix up the intake and exhaust rockers (although this will be physically impossible on many angle-valve heads anyway). Label everything and store the parts in a safe place.

At this point, you ought to be able to reach your fingers into the pushrod housings and withdraw the loose rods. Again, *don't get the two mixed up* (and don't reinstall them reversed end-to-end). Label the exhaust pushrod "exhaust"—and intake "intake"—and put the rods in a safe place. (If either one is visibly bowed or mushroomed, call in a mechanic at once.)

If you've gotten down on your hands and knees and studied the way Continental's pushrod housings are installed, you've no doubt noticed that each one is bound in place with a hell-for-stout spring. To remove a housing, you'll need to work against this spring—i.e., you'll have to push on the tube (from the cylinder head end) with a blunt tool of some sort, and *keep* pushing towards the crankcase until the outer end of the tube is clear of the cylinder head. Then you can let the tube drop out (or fly out and hit you in the groin, as the case may be).

As you catch the shroud tube, also catch that stout spring, and note the presence of a washer-seal-washer sandwich at either of the tube. If you don't see the complete sandwich, stop and look for the missing components. (It's not unusual for a steel washer to remain in the crankcase. Fish it out with you finger.) Obviously, you'll want to save the steel washers—and throw away the old seals.

Note: The silastic seals may either be red or white. There's no significance to the color; the red ones were predecessors of the whites, and if you've got red seals, it merely means your engine hasn't been overhauled since LBJ days.

New pushrod housing seals can be obtained through your local FBO, or from Precision Air Parts, P.O. Box 336, Wetumpka, AL 36092. The Continental price is 85 cents each; Precision's price is 25 cents apiece. (For most Continental engines, the part number is 534610.) You'll need four seals, obviously, per cylinder, since there are two seals per housing and two housings per jug.

To install new seals, just put a new washer-seal-washer sandwich at either end of each pushrod housing, slide the stout spring onto the "tappet" end of the housing as before, and (inserting the housing first into the crankcase, then into the cylinder head) reinstall everything in the reverse order of disassembly.

There's a catch, of course: Getting that big spring compressed (and keeping it compressed while you install the shroud) isn't easy. There are two preferred ways of dealing with this. One way is to compress the spring in a vise, then safety-wire it in the compressed condition—and slide it onto the shroud for reassembly to the engine. (Once everything is in place on the engine, you can snip the safety wire with a pair of dikes, and presto! The shroud is spring-loaded in place.) Another way of going at this is to use a special tool to compress the spring (and keep it compressed). One such tool we've used—the most popular one for this purpose in the industry—is the GS-221 pushrod installer by Gibson Aviation, P.O. Box 880, El Reno, OK 73036 (phone 405/262-48880). The GS-221 (and the -221A, for IO-360 Continentals) costs $32.50, including shopping. This tool is pictured in the accompanying photographs.

Admittedly, it takes a little practice to load (perhaps "arm" would be a better work) the Gibson spring compressor. But the result is worth it. With the spring loaded into the Gibson tool, you are free to install the spring/housing/seal-sandwich onto the cylinder with one hand. And when the whole affair has been positioned properly under the jug, you simply yank the Gibson tool out, and whang! The shroud is spring-loaded in place.

It's extremely important, in any case, that after you reinstall any housing you doublecheck it for proper "fit" at both ends. Compare it with neighboring jugs' shroud tubes. The idea is to be sure the washers are fully seated (and centered on their seats.) Ask a mechanic for help if you're not sure what you're looking at. (You'll need an A&P's look-see anyway, if you want to remain legal.)

With the housings and new seals in place, all that remains is to insert the pushrods in their proper tunnels (dip them in oil first, and be sure the oil feed holes in the ball ends are open); put the rockers on their repspective shafts; slide the rocker shafts back into their proper places; reinstall and rocker shaft retainer bolts (check your engine service manual for proper torque—if you overtorque these bolts you stnd a good chance of setting up cracks in the rocker boss ears); and safety the bolts before putting the valve cover back on (with a fresh gasket). Be sure safety-wire is run in a *tightening* direction, as shown in the photo.

Finally, no job of this sort should be considered complete until a ground runup (and visual leak check) is conducted, to make sure that in the process of trying to fix a drip you haven't somehow created a gusher.

When everything check out okay, make appropriate log entries—and congratulate yourself on accomplishing a $30 to $60 job (and doing it right) for $2.00.

OVERSPEEDING

Overspeeding results in a variety of ills, broken valve springs being a classic example. All it takes is a moment's hesitation during recovery from an unusual attitude; or poor throttle control in a lazy-8, wingover, loop, or departure stall; or sudden failure of the prop governor (in a constant-speed-prop aircraft),to make the tachometer needle surge past redline. The question is: Then what? Inspectionwise, what should a pilot (or mechanic) be prepared to look for in case of an unexpected overspeed?

First, it's important to clarify exactly what constitutes "overspeeding." Continental considers that overspeeding doesn't begin until the engine rpm exceeds redline for more than 10 seconds; then, depending on how far beyond redline the tach went, the exact engine model, and other factors, various types of inspections may or may not be required (more of which in a minute). Lycoming takes a slightly different view: Lycoming defines "momentary overspeed" as operation for not more than three seconds at speeds not exceeding 110 percent of normal redline. According to Lycoming, all such momentary events—precisely because they are so short-lived (and limited as to rpm)—can be ignored for maintenance purposes.

But Lycoming takes a much different view of non-momentary overspeeds—that is, any overrev of more than 110 percent of redline (no matter the duration), or over 100 percent but lasting more than three seconds. Any overspeed of this nature is considered significant enough to warrant further inspection. (In cases where an engine has a 5-minute takeoff rating, as well as a max-continuous rpm, the takeoff rpm is considered the basis for overspeed computations.)

So if you have a Lycoming engine, and you find yourself coming out of an unusual-attitude recovery with the nose pointing straight down and your hand frozen on the throttle (and the rpm sailing past redline), the first thing you do—back on the ground—is calculate how many percent beyond redline the engine went. If less than five percent (e.g., 140 rpm for an O-235 redlined at 2,800), you can simply make a logbook notation and forget about it, if it's a direct-drive (non-geared) engine. (If you have a mechanically supercharged Lycoming, such as a GSO-480 or IGSO-540, the factory advises that you remove the supercharger drain cover to look for engine oil seeping past the supercharger seal. If more than a teaspoonful of oil drains from this area, replace the blower seal. See Lycoming Service Bulletin No. 369.)

Geared engines (and helicopter engines) normally run at much higher speeds than direct-drive engines, of course. But the engine manufacturers take special care to increase design margins in such engines with regard to major reciprocating parts (including valve springs, rods, rod bolts, and pistons). Hence, the rpm limits for geared engines (and helicopter engines) are not comparable to those for direct-drive engines of equivalent displacement. What holds true for an HIO-360 does not hold true for the typical IO-360, because the HIO-engine differs with respect to critical components.

For overspeeds of from five percent to ten percent beyond redline, Lycoming recommends inspection of oil filters and screens for metal; a differential compression check of all cylinders; borescope inspection of all cylinders to detect possible barrel scoring from broken rings (and valve-seat damage); a visual check of valve springs for damage; and complete overhaul of both magnetos (with a check of magneto drive gears for looseness). In addition, you should turn the prop by hand (very carefully) and observe the rockers for equal lift on all valves. (Also, comply with Lycoming Service Bulletin No. 388A on valve/guide clearances; see The Engine Clinic, *LPM*, April '87.)

Turbocharged models: Check the above items plus turbo rotor free play limits. (Supercharged models: Again, check the blower drain area for oil seepage.)

For overspeeds of more than 110 percent of redline (for any duration), Lycoming recommends a teardown of the engine and replacement of connecting rod bolts, valves, keepers, and all normal major-overhaul components.

Continental separates required overspeed actions into three categories, based on peak rpm reached: Category One overspeeds are defined as those in which rpm did not exceed 2,900 for 470-series engines, or 3,000 rpm for all other non-geared Continentals (or 3,500 rpm for GTSIO-series powerplants). Category Two overspeeds are considered to be those for which the peak rpm went above the limits just stated, but not higher than 3,200 for 470-series, 3,700 geared, and 3,300 rpm for all others. Category Three takes in any overspeed of more than 3,200, 3,700, or 3,300 rpm (as appropriate to the engine family), and—you guessed it—a major overhaul is the bitter medicine prescribed for this category. (Continental recommends total replacement of connecting rods—not just rod bolts—during an "overspeedhaul," which certainly makes sense for IO-360, TSIO-360, IO-520, TSIO-520, and geared engines.)

As to remedial action for the other categories: Category One events require no action, if the overspeed's duration was less than 10 seconds. (One would assume that the 10-second allowance is cumulative over the TBO life of the engine.) If it was in excess of 10 seconds, simply drain oil and check all screens/filters; check accessory drives for backlash (in accordance with the appropriate Overhaul Manual); and remove all rocker covers to allow visual inspection of valve tips, springs, retainers, rotators, rocker arms, and pushrods and lifters. If no damage is evident, repeat the inspection in five hours, then make a log entry and forget about it.

Category Two overspeeds require somewhat more stringent procedures (naturally): If less than 10 seconds' total duration, simply carry out the checks just described (Category One above); if more than 10 seconds, remove all cylinders (plus all rods and pistons) for top overhaul. Discard all rod bolts. Further, remove all dynamic counterweights and replace C/W pins and bushings as necessary. Make the necessary log notations indicating which components were inspected and found good, and which were replaced; then return the engine to service.

For further information, consult Teledyne Continental Service Bulletin M87-9, dated April 30, 1987 (superseding M75-16) or call the factory at 205/438-3411. (See also Lycoming S.B. 369, or call the Williamsport factory at 717/323-6181.)

The message is clear: Overspeeding is primarily harmful to reciprocating components (rods, valve train, piston rings), counterweights (and their bushings), and geared components (accessory drives and, if applicable, propeller drive). In addition, accessories themselves should come in for close scrutiny, particularly magnetos and vacuum pumps. In six-cylinder engines, magnetos run at one-and-a-half times crankshaft speed, while in four-bangers the mags run at crank speed. And dry vacuum pumps—generally rated for 4,000 rpm, maximum—run at different speeds on different engines: 1.3 times crank speed on Lycomings, and 1.5 times crank speed on Continentals. Any significant overspeed of a Lycoming or Continental engine should mean replacement of the vacuum pump, if it is of the dry kind.

Chapter 3

COLD-WEATHER SAFEGUARDS

Until new airplanes come equipped with (and until about 150,000 *old* airplanes are retrofitted with) block heaters, multiple batteries, and the like, pilots are going to continue to have a bit of trouble starting their engines in cold weather, and the less cautious among us will continue to score cylinder walls, scuff pistons, break piston rings, etc., as we coax our reluctant engines into coming to life. Since it has been estimated that between 50% and 90% of all cylinder wear takes place during the first one to two minutes following startup—and since cold-weather starting is (or can be) much harder on an engine than warm-weather starting—it can logically be said that, in the cold-weather months, preventive engine maintenance begins with adherance to proper engine starting technique.

There are many ways of getting an engine started in moderately cold weather (temperatures down to, say, 10°F); not all of them are good for one's engine, however. All that's needed to start any piston engine (at any temperature) is fuel vapor in the cylinders in sufficient quantity, and adequate cranking power to rev the engine (and generate a spark). Thus, to start an engine in cold weather, all you have to do—if you want to be crude about it—is generously prime the engine, connect an extra battery to the plane's electrical system with a set of jumper cables, and start cranking. Never mind the fact that after the first two seconds of priming, you've washed the oil off of at least part of the cylinder walls, exposing bare metal. Never mind the fact that if the oil hasn't been preheated (or its viscosity modified in some way), the oil will not be able to flow fast enough to keep up with those rapidly moving piston rings once the engine starts. Cylinder walls and piston pins are, in most engines, spray-lubricated by oil escaping for connecting-rod bearings. You can imagine the kind of "spray" that is produced when stone-cold 30-weight or 40-weight oil is circulating through the engine.

If you are using straight 30-weight (or 40-weight) av oil in your engine, you should forget about using the "brute force" method of starting a cold engine when the temperature dips below about 24°F. *Above* 25°F, if you adhere to proper starting technique (see discussion below), you can get by with massive priming and cold cranking. (We're not saying that you *can't succeed in starting* a cold-but-well-primed-enging below 25°F, using just battery power . . . rather, from a preventive maintenance standpoint, we're saying it's *unwise* to cold-start an engine below 25°F. Piston ring breakage is a possibility above 25°F; below 25°F, it's a likelihood.

The above rule of thumb, mind you, is for engines in which a single-grade 30 or 40-weight av oil is being used. The situation changes dramatically (for the better) if you use a multiviscosity "all season" aviation oil, such as Phillips's X/C 20W-50 av oil, Mobil AV-1, or Aeroshell W Multigrade, the 15W-50 version of the popular Aero W 100. Any of these oils will give you excellent cold-cranking performance (and good protection against ring breakage, cylinder scoring, etc.) down to about 10°F. Below 10°F, preheating should be considered mandatory (regardless of oil type), if insurance against engine damage is desired.

Operators should switch to one of the aforementioned multigrade av oils as soon as possible, if low-temperature operations are being conducted. Because these oils are true multigrades, they will not-undergo excessive thinning (viscosity loss) at normal engine operating temperatures, as SAE20 or 30 single grade oils will. The new miltigrades flow very readily at low temperatures (Shell's 15W-50 oil has a pour point of minus 30°F); thus, not only is easier engine startup assured, but the need for long warmups prior to takeoff is eliminated. The minute you start your engine, you've got "warm oil" oil pressure indications (no waiting for the needle to come down from redline); you've got prop governor action (no waiting for congealed oil to warm up); you've got a properly functioning turbo wastegate controller; and (very important) your hydraulic lifters—if you have them—operate normally as you open the throttle for takeoff. These are all important considerations.

No matter what type of oil you use, successful (no damage) cold-starting depends on close adherence to a couple of rules. Number one, prime the engine generously *in accordance with the precise instructions given in your engine operator's manual.* (If you don't have one of these manuals, write to the engine manufacturer and get one.) If the book says to use six shots of primer, use six shots of primer...and press the primer plunger forcefully, to maximize atomization of the fuel.

Number two, pull the prop through several revolutions between each shot of primer, to redistribute oil on the cylinder walls and aid in vaporization of the fuel. (*CAUTION: Treat the propeller as if it is "hot"...because it may well be, if either of your magneto's P-leads is broken or improperly connected. Be sure the plane is tied down, the keys are in your pocket, and your footing is steady. And even then, be ready in case the engine fires. Naturally, you'll want the mixture control in the idle cutoff position, to prevent continued engine operation in the event of a sudden start.*) You'll be surprised what a difference this makes in ease of cold-starting.

If you have a carburetor-equipped plane, leave the throttle cracked only a minimal amount (this will cause the butterfly to act as a choke)—and be ready to prime the engine as it starts up. A slow, additional prime is often necessary before and immediately after the first cough of life, to keep the engine going. Alternatively, you can pump the throttle vigorously to get extra fuel to the cylinders—but this is a less exact way of metering the fuel. (You can at least control the speed at which you push the primer plunger down; it is much harder to modulate fuel flow through throttle oscillations...particularly when you consider that a certain fraction of the raw fuel exuded by the carburetor is going to drip out onto the ground, due to the unit's updraft positioning. With a primer system, fuel is delivered straight to the cylinders.)

By the way, if your plane is outfitted with a *single-cylinder* type of primer system...we can only advise strongly that you buy a conversion kit to give your priming system multiple-cylinder capability. There's no point at all in having just one jug out of our (or six) start up on a cold morning, while the others scrape their way to an early overhaul. Single-cylinder priming systems are on a par with single-lens sunglasses and single-wheel braking systems. They're worse than no system at all.

Once the properly primed engine is running, it is vital that it be kept running. During the first revolutions of the engine, enough water is formed in combustion to cuase serious icing-over of spark plug electrodes if the engine stops running. (It takes 30 or 40 power strokes for set of 0°F electrodes to warm up to above freezing temperature.) Once the electrodes are iced over, nothing short of direct heat will thaw them and get them working again.

To keep the engine running, it may be necessary (as mentioned before) to reapply primer or stroke the throttle. Another trick that works well is to apply carburetor heat (if you have that capability) immediately after startup. Exhaust gases are hot enough to provide carb heat almost immediately. The heat will, in turn, do two things:

[1] By decreasing the density of the incoming air, extra-rich fuel mixture conditions will be created...which is just what's needed on a frigid morning when the air is very cold, very dense, and thus very rich in oxygen.

[2] Fuel vaporization will be aided, improving overall combustion, but also improving the distribution of fuel (and tetraethyl lead, and lead scavengers) to all the cylinders. In the absence of some kind of preheat, vaporization of aviation gasoline takes place slowly or not at all in cold weather, since all aviation gasolines are (unlike automotive gas) purposely blended to have a very low vapor pressure.

Note: Once the engine comes to life, it is *extremely* important not to rev the engine to more than 1500 rpm. Crankshaft rpm should be kept below 1200 rpm, if possible. Sudden revving of the engine while it is cold can cause piston scuffing, cylinder scoring, and/or ring breakage, not to mention oil pump cavitation (cold oil does not pump well).

In any cold start, with any aircraft engine, there is alwyas a danger of fire, since a great deal of liquid fuel is sent to the cylinders to create a small amount of combustible vapor. It is highly advisable that a portable fire extinguisher be kept in the plane during cold-weather starts. In the event of an engine fire, your first action should be to *continue cranking the engine* so as to suck the fire out and away from the carburetor (if carburetor-equipped); if this fails to kill the fire, or if it is obvious that liquid fuel has spread a fire throughout the engine compartment, your next action is to *shut off the fuel* to the carburetor or injector...and exit the plane, extinguisher in hand. Don't sit in the plane trying to rouse somebody on Unicom; if there's anyone nearby, they'll be able to see that you need help, without your calling them on radio.

From personal experience, we can vouch for the efficacy of small, powder-type extinguishers in putting out carburetor fires.

If you have—or even suspect that you may have had—a carburetor fire, or an engine fire of any kind, ground the aircraft immediately (once the fire is out); do not proceed to go flying. There are cases on record of pilots experiencing in-flight carburetor trouble due to melting of carburetor components during previous start attempts. In some cases, the pilots never knew that they had had an engine fire in the first place. A thorough inspection of the engine and induction system should be undertaken if a fire has occurred (or is suspected to have occurred).

From a preventive-maintenance standpoint, engine preheat can only be considred cheap insurance against cold-start-related engine damage—even if you end up having to pay your FBO $5 to $10 (or even more) per warmup. Which, of course, you don't *have* to do; you can always invest in your own preheating rig. (*Trade-A-Plane* always contains some ads by companies selling aircraft preheaters.) The trouble with most of the preheaters being sold on the aircraft atermarket these days is [1] they're expensive—usually $300 or more—and [2] they require 110-volt alternating current, which may not be available if you're tied down out on the ramp, a quarter mile from the nearest hangar. If you have access to 110-volt a.c., you certainly don't need one of those $300 propane-burners to get your engine warm; a 98¢ light bulb placed in close proximity to the oil sump overnight will do the job, in most cases. Failing that, a cheap electric hair-dryer will do wonders. Aim the end of the dryer alternately at the oil sump, the induction manifold, and the crankcase breather. (If ice has frozen in your breather, preventing your engine from breathing . . . and you don't remove that ice before your next flight . . . you stand a good chance of blowing the front main bearing seal out of your engine on your next takeoff.) If access to the battery is good, blow some hot air on it, too, and your engine will crank a bit more vigorously when the Moment of Truth comes.

Some pilots have taken to running a piece of hot-air ducting from their car exhaust pipe to the engine compartment of their airplane as a means of providing preheat to the latter. This is not a good idea by any stretch of the imagination. Engine exhaust is highly corrosive . . . particularly the sulfur-laden exhaust that comes out of a catalytic-converter-equipped late-seventies American vehicle. Sulfur dioxide and sulfuric acid are both present in significant amounts in the exhaust of late-model cars; both will rot fuel hoses (and oil hoses) very quickly. Ozone, of course, is also present in exhaust fumes, and you know what ozone does to rubber. Don't blow car exhaust into your cowling.

A better idea for capturing the heat given off by a *car's* engine to heat an *airplane's* engine (if needed you believe that's a reasonable thing to try to do in the first place) is to rig ducting from the car's heater outlets and run the ducts into your cowl. Someone—we don't know who—offers a kit with instructions on how to do this . . . at a cost of about $300. Tanis Aircraft Services, P.O. Box 117, Glenwood, MN 56334 markets an unusual (and unusually effective) preheating system for Lycoming and Continental engines—the TAS system—wherein tiny heat probes (one per cylinder) are connected to the engine, along with a "hot" oil drain plug (two plugs for 470 and 520 Continentals). The system is inexpensive—about $300 for four-cylinder engines, somewhat more for sixes—as well as lightweight (about two pounds), and supposedly can be installed by the owner in two hours. The only catch is that 110-volt a.c. is required to operated the system.

If you end up buying your preheats from an FBO, we strongly suggest you supervise the heating operation yourself. Remember that too much heat can be worse than no heat at all, particularly when the heat is directed at fuel injector components (which may contain meltable parts). Also remember that the idea is not to heat the cylinders, but the oil…and, to a lesser extent, the induction manifold. Thus, you'll want to be sure that the heater hoses are directed at the *oil sump*, if possible, and only part of the time at the cylinders. If you have cowl flaps, alternate between putting the heater ducts in the cowl flaps and placing them in the front of the cowl. Alternate back and forth, 5 or 10 minutes at each location, for a total of 15 minutes minimum (but preferably 20 or 30 minutes). If possible, pull the prop through several times during the warmup period, to aid the distribution of heat throughout the oil supply.

Opinions vary on whether or not one should leave the cowl flaps closed after engine startup, prior to takeoff on a cold morning. Some people insist that if the cowl flaps are left closed, "hot spots" will develop in the engine compartment during warmup, resulting in cooked hoses, fried ignition wires, etc. Our own opinion (for non-turbocharged aircraft) is that when the temperature is below approximately 5° to 10°, it can't hurt to leave the flaps closed for ten minutes or so after engine start.

Oil dilution systems—in which gasoline is diverted (by means of a hand-operated knob) from the main fuel strainer to the crankcase or oil sump, to thin the oil immediately prior to engine shutdown—are installed on many light aircraft (including many single-engine Cessnas), and can be retrofitted to older aircraft. Oil dilution is merely a primitive way of lowering cold oil's viscosity (by mixing gasoline with it). During startup on a cold day, the diluted oil flows easily; then, when it reaches normal operating temperature, the volatile gasoline molecules in the oil boil off and pass out the crankcase breather. At the

Camshaft damage is among the commonest forms of oil-starvation damage on cold startups (particularly with Lycoming engines). This cam lobe is severely worn due to lube failure. The pilot preheated the cylinders only, neglecting the crankcase and sump.

end of the next flight, the oil is diluted (by the pilot pulling a knob), and the oil is thus thinned in preparation for the next cold start. And so on.

The trouble with oil dilution is that during the warm months of the year, the plane may fly several hundred hours—and the engine, consequently, may form a considerable (but normal) amount of sludge. When cold weather comes, and oil dilution is used for the first time in several hundred hours, some of this accumulated sludge and carbon can be dislodged by the diluted oil and carried downsteam in the oil system, ultimately to lodge in system screens, thereby perhaps causing oil pump cavitation and/or an interruption in engine lubrication. The latter could be quite costly.

The thing to do, if you have an oil dilution system and you worry about problems with sludge (you should), is to dilute your oil immediately prior to each oil change throughout the year. (Do this while the oil is still hot.) Shut the engine down as soon as the oil has been diluted the proper amount (check your owner's manual), then change oil and inspect the sump screens. Your screens (and/or your oil filter element) should tell you the whole story as far as sludge problems go. Dilute and change your oil every 25 hours in this fashion, and you'll prevent sludge from building up in the engine.

If you don't have an oil dilution system—and you don't have access to engine preheat—there's only one safe way to get your engine started in extreme cold: Take the oil out and heat it (and/or *dilute* it). Cessna, in its 1963 to 1968 100 *Series Service Manual*, advises operators to proceed as follows (for both Lycoming and Contenental engines):

"After the last flight of the day, drain the engine oil into a clean container so the oil can be preheated. Cover the engine to prevent ice or snow from collecting inside the cowling. When preparing the aircraft for flight or engine runup after these conditions have been followed, preheat the drained oil. After preheating the oil, gasoline may be mixed with the oil in a ratio of 1 part gasoline to 12 parts oil before pouring into the engine oil sump. If the free air temperature is below -20°F (-29°C), the engine compartment should [also] be preheated by a ground heater. After the engine compartment has been reheated, inspect all engine compartment drain and vent lines for presence of ice. After this procedure has been followed, pull the propeller through several revolutions by hand before starting the engine."

Note: If you decide to follow the above procedure, be sure not to heat the oil above 121°C (250°F), since a flash fire could result. Also, observe the proper safety precautions whenever pulling a propeller through by hand.

The same caution about sludge clogging problems mentioned above applies to owners of non-diluter-equipped aircraft who try the

Turbocharged engines should not be run at full power until the oil-temperature needle is off the peg and well into the green. Turbo controllers and wastegates are oil-actuated, and thick oil may mean momentary overboosting.

foregoing Cessna dilution/preheat procedure. Any time you dilute your oil (in some cases, even with other, thinner oil), you stand a chance of dislodging sludge and carbon deposits...deposits that can create problems elsewhere in the engine. So watch the oil-pressure gauge closely after you start your engine using diluted oil. If obvious, noticeable fluctuations appear in the engine's oil pressure during engine warmup, shut the engine down immediately and pull all the oil screens (and the filter, if any). Clean all the screens, install a new oil filter, and service the engine with fresh oil before attempting a restart. And then, again, watch the oil pressure closely.

A final word of advice: If you anticipate prolonged operation in cold temperatures, by all means order the appropriate cold-weather kit for your aircraft. (Most aircraft models have a factory-approved cold weather, or "winterization", kit. It consists mostly of baffles to restrict airflow around the engine and/or the oil cooler.) But don't keep the cold-weather baffles on for flights into warm-temperature regions. Take them off well before the spring thaw.

FUEL-SYSTEM ICE

Water's solubility in gasoline is very low, but it is not zero. Some water inevitably "stays behind" after a sump drain, but normally the tiny amount of water suspended in a tank of fuel is not sufficient to cause power interruption (because we're talking very tiny amounts of water indeed). But in extremely cold conditions, suspended water molecules become suspended ice granules. And under certain conditions, such ice particles can accumulate in the flow divider or delivery lines of a fuel-injected aircraft, causing engine stoppage.

Teledyne Continental Motors announced a special "Oil Heated Fuel Manifold Valve Retrofit Kit" for TSIO-520-J, K, N/NB, GTSIO-520-D, H, and L engines in October 1984 (see Customer Information Bulletin CIB 84-4). Cessna announced the change in Service Letter ME84-37. Continental instituted a program at the same time under which purchasers of TCM factory-rebuilt engines of the above models can specify oil-heated injector manifolds at no extra charge. Obviously, the factory wants people to take advantage of the mod.

The Continental modification takes starboard-gallery pressure oil from between cylinders 3 and 5 of the GTSIO-520 (or from the oil cooler of TSIO-520 models mentioned above) and routes it to a shroud around the injector spider (flow divider) atop the engine. Return oil then goes to the crankcase via a tube to the timing hole plug. From the design of the system, it would seem that Cessna and Continental have determined that ice can form in the fuel injection delviery lines and/ or the injector spider, unless the fuel is heated (with hot engine oil). Certainly, this is where the fuel would be coldest, on its way to the cylinders. The rush of cooling air through the cowling is unobstructed here, and the wind chill factor at FL 250 (where the air is minus-30 on a standard day), at Cessna 421 cruising speeds, has to be substantial.

Although the above modification applies only to engines for Cessna 340, 414, and 421 aircraft, the problem of ice-crystal formation in fuel at high altitude potentially affects every operator of a turbocharged aircraft. The solution needn't involve oil heating, however. Prist (generically: EGME) is approved for use in piston engine aircraft, at concentrations up to 0.15 percent. (Approval is by engine and airframe manufacturer service bulletin; no STC paperwork is required.)

A member of the glycol family, Prist's active ingredient, ethylene glycol monomethyl ether, is only barely soluble in gasoline, but it is

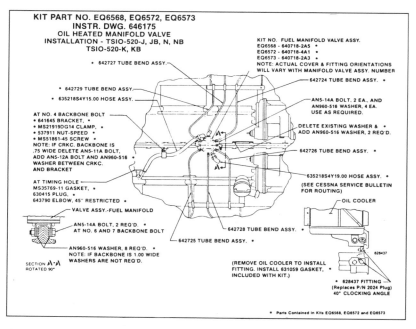

Continental offers a retrofit kit to provide an oil-heated injector manifold on its TSIO-520 and GTSIO-520 engines, as shown in this diagram. The purpose of the kit is to prevent ice crystals from forming in the manifold at high altitudes.

highly soluble in water. At low temperatures, when water droplets separate from fuel, Prist leaves the fuel to preferentially dissolve in the water, depressing its freezing point. As the fuel gets colder and more water microdroplets appear, more Prist leaves the fuel and enters the water, essentially keeping the water from forming ice crystals at all OATs that can be encountered by piston aircraft.

Prist also has antimicrobial properties, but microbe growth in aviation gasoline is not a problem (in contrast to Jet A).

Properties of Prist (EGME)	
Approval	FAA AC 20-133
	MIL-I-27686E
	ASTM D4171-82
Density (lbs/gal)	8.03
Specific gravity	.963
Molecular weight	76.1
Flash point (°F)	107
Specific heat	0.534
Freezing pt.	-85.1°C
Boiling pt.	123.5°C
Vapor pressure (mm Hg)	6.2
Water, %	0.15

Prist is typically dispersed in fuel via aerosol-can application at the time of refueling. And until recently, Prist spray cans were "calibrated" for flow rates typical of Jet A fueling equipment. Now, however, Prist aerosol is available in a special Lo-Flo dispenser for use with avgas. One 8-ounce can treats approximately 90 gallons of gas.

Prist, incidentally, is a registered trademanrk of PPG Industries, makers of Durethane paints. For more information, request bulletin 1276B-5M-686, "Prist Aviation Fuel Additive," from PPG Industries, Inc., One PPG Place, Pittsburgh, PA 15272. (To order, see your FBO, or telephone PPG at 1-800-245-2974 or 412/434-3131.

ALTERNATE AIR

As any 100-hour private pilot knows, the principal advantage of fuel injection—aside from the ability to precisely meter fuel (if not air) to each cylinder—is immunity to venturi ice. With fuel injection, flight in "visible moisture" (translate: flight inside clouds—IFR flying) doesn't result in carburetor ice. IFR operations can be conducted with total peace of mind, where induction ice is concerned. In theory, at least.

In practice, flying "hard IFR" in an injected aircraft can lead to unnecessary inflight excitement, if you don't know how your alternate-air system works. This message was recently underscored by

Some planes' alternate air controls are manual (as in the case of the Seneca II installation shown here). It's important to see that the alternate air door remains tightly closed when not in use.

Piper Service Letter No. 900 (dated November 17, 1986), sent to all Malibu owners. The letter says (in part):

"Reports have been received of aircraft losing manifold pressure during flight in clouds, particularly at altitudes above 18,000 feet. Engineering tests confirm that this can occur . . . [and suggest methods] to lessen or prevent this condition."

"Ice buildup on the induction air filter in the primary induction system," the Piper letter goes on, "is a predominant cause of manifold pressure loss in clouds. This condition can occur even with no evidence of ice buildup on other portions of the aircraft. [Moreover], this phenomenon is particularly prevalent at flight above 18,000 feet." (Our italics.)

In the Piper Malibu (powered by a Continental TSIO-520-BE), alternate air is manually controlled by the pilot. The pilot can wait until induction ice is encountered—signified by a loss of manifold pressure—or he/she can apply alternate air prophylactically, as desired. Not all fuel-injected aircraft are set up this way, however. In fact, the diversity of "alt air" installations (and descriptions of same in Pilots' Operating Handbooks) is truly impressive. For example:

—The 1975 Cessna 210 has a suck-open air door that deploys automatically when the air filter becomes obstructed. According to the POH, "a decrease of 1 to 2 inches full-throttle manifold pressure" will result.

—The P210N has a suck-open door (upstream of the turbo) bypassing the air filter, the deployment of which "will result in a decrease of up to 10 inches Hg manifold pressure from a cruise-power setting." (Our emphasis.)

—The Piper Turbo Arrow IV (Continental TSIO-360-FB engine) has a suck-open door upstream of the turbo compressor that opens automatically in case of filter blockage; but alternate air can be manually deployed from the cockpit as well. The POH makes no comment about manifold pressure loss.

—The Piper Arrow III (Lycoming IO-360-C1C6) has an alternate air door that opens automatically or manually; no information given in the POH concerning manifold pressure loss.

—The Piper Turbo Saratoga (Lycoming TIO-540-S1AD) has two alternate air doors, one manual and the other a suck-open type downstream of the turbo compressor. No discussion is made in the POH of manifold pressure loss, but since the suck-open door bypasses the turbocharger, an extreme MP loss would almost certainly have to accompany automatic door opening, and from that point on the engine would be normally aspirated.

—The 1977 Cessna Hawk XP has a suck-open door with no manual control; its opening causes "negligible variations in manifold pressure," according to Cessna's handbook.

—The Mooney 201 (Lycoming IO-360-A3B6D) has a spring-loaded suck-open door (non-pilot-controllable) situated between the air filter and the separate ram-air door (which is pilot-controllable). In the event of air filter blockage, the suck-open door opens automatically, allowing unfiltered air into the engine. But the pilot can also select ram air at the same time. In fact, if the air filter clogs and the "alt air" door freezes shut, the pilot can still get alternate air to the engine via the ram-air control alone; and rather than manifold pressure going down, the MP may actually increase ion this situation—a unique arrangement, as small planes go.

—The Piper Aztec F has manual as well as suck-open alternate air doors. The manual door is upstream of the turbo. No mention is made of manifold pressure loss.

—The Beech V35B (D-9948 and after; Continental IO-520-B engine) has a spring-loaded alternate air door designed to open automatically. The pilot is provided with a T-handle in the cockpit, however. Says the POH: "If the alternate air source door becomes frozen in the closed position, a pull-and-release T-handle is provided to force the door open." (No mention of manifold pressure loss.)

—The Beech Baron B55 (TC-1608 and on; Continental IO-470-L) has suck-open alternate air with no pilot control. The POH does not mention manifold pressure loss.

Dearth of Advice

In examining the Pilots' Operating Handbooks for the above aircraft, we could not find a single instance in which the manual gave practical advice on the use of alternate air in clouds above 18,000 feet. The closest any manufacturer has gotten to providing detailed information on this subject is Piper Service Letter No. 900, which advises Malibu owners as follows:

"[We] recommend the use of alternate induction air whenever induction system icing is suspected or a loss of manifold pressure is observed, and prior to entering clouds at altitudes above 18,000 feet. A drop in manifold pressure can be expected when operating on alternate induction air at high altitude due to the loss of ram air pressure in the primary induction system. The magnitude of the loss will vary depending on altitude and outside air temperature. It may be possible to recover part or all of the manifold pressure loss by advancing the throttle and re-leaning the engine . . . . "Upon exiting the clouds, it may not be possible to regain manifold pressure until accumulated filter ice has melted. If manifold pressure drops when primary air is selected, the induction air control should be left in alternate until the outside air temperature is above freezing." (Piper's emphasis.)

Most manuals make no mention of the fact that alternate air doors are capable of freezing shut in precisely the conditions that warrant their use. (Beech is an exception; see the V35B owner's manual.) Pilots should be alert to this possibility when ascending through rain, drizzle, or freezing rain (or wet snow) to a final altitude above the freezing level. The only way to prevent the alternate air door from freezing shut in such conditions is to open it manually ahead of time.

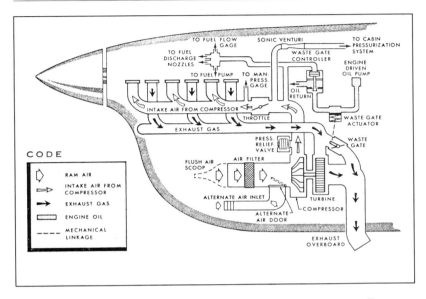

The Cessna P210 alternate air door is upstream of the turbo compressor. Even so, a loss of as much as 10 inches of manifold pressure is possible when alternate air is used in flight. It's extremely important to read and understand the applicable POH, and heed the warnings contained therein.

Prophylactic use of "alt air" in IMC is coming to be considered essential by operators of certain aircraft—such as the Mooney 231 and Cessna Turbo 310/320—which seem to be unusually susceptible to induction system blockage. A Cessna 320 operator in the Pacific Northwest who has experienced double engine failure as a result of filter obstruction in IMC at high altitude told us: "I got so concerned about the situation, I wrote to every 320 operator on FAA's registry. I heard back from most of them, and was surprised to learn that many owners are flying without air filters in the winter months. Others have adopted a technique of applying full alternate air before entering a cloud. If you wait until after you enter the cloud, it's too late."

Mooney Testing

In March 1984, Mooney sent a test pilot to Alberta, Canada to fly with a 231 owner in search of high-altitude induction ice. The owner and the test pilot went up in one aircraft; a pair of local pilots went up in a second Mooney 231. "We were just skimming the stratocu tops when the other aircraft reported significant power losses due to induction icing. We turned towards their location and descended to FL 190, which immediately put us into cloud. Within 45 seconds, we lost eight inches of MP as we flew through the ice crystals at minus-24 degrees C." (There was no airframe icing.)

After an additional two-inch drop in manifold pressure, alternate air was selected, but power did not increase. The owner relates the story: "As our airspeed was decaying, we went to full rich and max rpm"—the throttle was already wide-open—"and this allowed us to maintain altitude, but with 20 to 30 knots less airspeed than before." Eventually, the plane passed through the ice-crystal-laden cloud, and MP slowly began to pick up.

Mooney's test flights in Alberta (with two customer airplanes, plus a highly instrumented factory 231) led to several conclusions, among them:

1. Induction filter icing is most likely to occur in ice-crystal clouds below minus-20 Celsius, or in heavy snow. Even so, predictability is difficult. When cloud moisture is "wet" (conducive to airframe icing), the moisture droplets tend to resist right-angle turns in the intake ducting (due to inertia effects) and impact the corners of the ducts, rather than accumulating on the air filter.

2. Due to radiant heat from the 231's turbocharger, it is impossible to have induction icing downstream of the filter.

3. Alternate air is unfiltered air. But even with the alternate air door open, the engine is getting some residual air flow through the partially blocked off filter. Therefore, some additional manifold pressure loss can still occur after alternate air is selected, as the filter continues to ice over.

4. On pre-1984 Mooney M20K (231) aircraft, maximum power with a fully blocked air filter (and alternate air selected) is sufficient to allow level flight at FL 190, but IAS will be not far from stall speed. At 13,000 feet, 60 percent power can be achieved with total air filter blockage, but to do this requires full throttle and max rpm. Thus, in an induction-ice situation, airspeed and range may be affected dramatically. ATC should be advised accordingly.

5. The 1984 Mooney 231 alternate air system draws air from a cooler spot (and through a larger opening), so altitude performance is 3,000 to 4,000 feet better than on earlier models. In addition, the 1984 system incorporates an alternate-air door that will automatically actuate if the pilot does not use the cockpit control. This system can be retrofitted to older aircraft under Mooney Service Instruction No. M20-71. Kit P/

N 940029-501 applies to aircraft S/Ns 25-001 thru -0446; kit -502 applies to S/Ns -0447 thru -0612; and kit -503 applies to S/Ns -0613 thru -0780. See your Mooney dealer for details.

Conclusion

As currently written, the Federal Aviation Regulations pertaining to alternate air systems on type-certificated aircraft (FAR 23.1091 and 23.1093) are such as to allow manufacturers to design any number of types of systems—and they do. Alternate air doors can be upstream or downstream of turbos (or both); they can be manually controllable, or automatic (or both); and despite the stricture in FAR 23.1091 that alternate air "may not result in a loss of excessive power," airplanes have been certificated with systems that cause as much as a 10-inch drop in manifold pressure (e.g., the Cessna P210N).

On top of all this, the manufacturers' operating handbooks are woefully inadequate when it comes to advising pilots of the proper use of alternate air. Few manuals specify the manifold pressure loss that can be expected on deployment of alternate air; fewer still make mention of the fact that suck-open doors can and do freeze shut in wet/cold weather conditions. Many manuals don't even give a schematic drawing of the system.

It's up to the pilot, then, to look under the cowling and learn the system. Is your alternate air door downstream of the turbo? Is it held closed by spring tension, or cable tension, or magnets—or possibly a combination of the three? (Is the magnet loose? The hinge pin corroded?) If your system is manual, how much manifold pressure loss occurs in normal cruise when "alt air" is selected? (Do some test-flying and find out.) Can your suck-open door be overridden? Can it be locked partway open, or must it be full-on or full-off? Does your engine require re-leaning after application of alternate air? How do the above considerations affect your plane's airspeed and range? These are installation-specific questions that only the individual owner can answer. And answer them you should; the alternative is to do your own inflight testing under bad-weather conditions, when you most need the information.

Part II

UNDERSTANDING POWER-AUGMENTING SYSTEMS

Chapter 4

TURBOCHARGING

Turbocharging is no longer the arcane subject it once was in general aviation, but most pilots' (and mechanics') knowledge of turbo design is only nitride-layer deep. Everybody knows that turbos for small planes come in two basic flavors—AiResearch and Rajay—and most pilots know that Rajays are physically small compared to Brand A. But ask a pilot anything else about turbos, and you're likely to get hot air for a response.

Rajay, incidentally, is not a company (anymore) but a brand name. The original Rajay was started in 1960 by Joe Leach and Ray Roseling. (It was Roseling's wife who conjured the anagram "Rajay.") The early turbos were fabricated for Rajay by the Thompson Valve Division of TRW, which also supplied the turbo for the Chevy Corvair. The Rajay line passed through several hands—including Jack Riley's and (most memorably) Rajay Industries of Long Beach—before winding up with Roto-Master in February 1982.

Rajay's earliest STC dates to 1961 with the Piper Apache. The first type certificate to approve a turbo for General Aviation use, however, was for the AiResearch-boosted Continental TSIO-470-B (approved September 9, 1960). The TSIO-470-B was used on the Cessna 320.

Today, Rajay turbos are found on more than 40 different aircraft types (some by STC, some by TC), including such popular models as the Piper Turbo Arrow, Seneca II/III, Turbo Aztec, Aerostar 601, and Rockwell Shrike. AiResearch turbos are found on all the blown Cessna twins (including the Turbo Skymasters), plus the Turbo Skylane, T- and P210, Piper's Navajo series, the Malibu, and all of Beech's boosted Barons, among other airplanes.

Physical Differences

With turbos, as with magnetos and engines, mechanics seem to be divided into two distinct camps. Some prefer Brand A; others (a minority, perhaps), Brand R. Question: Is there any real reason to prefer one brand over the other? Do the two makes differ significantly in design and/or construction?

There are some obvious physical differences. As mentioned above, all Rajay models are basically of the same physical size—i.e., very small. "The basic Rajay turbocharger," engineer Hugh MacInnes once told us, "falls into the same flow area as the AiResearch TO4B, but runs at a slightly lower speed to obtain the same manifold pressure." The Rajay 300E, with a 3-inch exducer, flows 400 to 700 cfm (cu. ft./min.) at 60,000 to 120,000 rpm. Installed weight is 15 pounds. (The 300E's counterpart, the AiResearch TO4, is used on the Turbo Skylane and the T303 Crusader, and in a dual-blower installation on the Piper Malibu.)

AiResearch offers a wide range of turbos, the largest being the T18 and TH08A models used on, for example, the Beech Duke and Cessna 421. These units weigh in at about 50 pounds each (installed) and produce as much flow as two Rajays, but at two-thirds the rpm.

So much for obvious differences. What about differences in design philosophy between Rajay and AiResearch? To the extent that such differences exist, what are the ramifications (if any) for reliability or repairability?

Floating Bearings

One of the main differences between the two brands has to do with bearing design. Obviously, any shaft turning upwards of 60,000 rpm is going to present unique problems for lubrication and bearing design. The first automotive turbos (predecessors of today's aircraft units) had stationary journal bearings which were pressed into the center housing in the manner of a low-speed bushing—a design that gave poor wear properties, even with internal water passages to keep the bearing temperature down. (Babbitt was frequently used as a bearing material, and unless there was a coolant jacket, the babbitt would melt after a hot shutdown.)

Today's turbochargers use either aluminum or bronze bearings (no babbitt) and water jackets are unnecessary. Almost all turbos now use a so-called floating bearing—a short, cylindrical sleeve with oil holes in it which, when slipped over the turbine shaft, protects the shaft from direct rubbing contact with the bearing housing. In other words, the sleeve, since it is free to rotate, offers the same clearance on the inside (between bearing and shaft) as on the outside (between bearing O.D. and housing I.D.), thus "cushioning" the shaft in two layers of oil film.

Floating bearings have all but eliminated metal-to-metal contact

Because of their high operating temperatures, most turbos are encased in protective foil or (as here) a stainless-steel heat shield. In the Cessna T310's turbo system, air enters a filter cannister (right) before going to compressor (middle); exhaust is expelled through turbine (left; note perforated shield) before going out the large exhaust pipe on the far left. Turbo is an AiResearch TE06.

between turbo shaft and center housings, with the result that turbo shaft materials needn't be nearly as hard as before. Instead of a journal hardness of Rockwell C60, today a journal hardness in the range of C35-40 is acceptable.

The only problem with floating bearings is that oil has to be fed through them (via circumferential holes) to get to the shaft. The reason this is a problem is that the bearings themselves rotate—in normal operation—at about half of shaft rpm, and in the process they act like miniature ultracentrifuges, slinging oil to the outside of the bearing. This oil "back pressure" must, of course, be overcome by pressure at the oil inlet line (i.e., by crankcase oil pressure). AiResearch, as a result, requires that oil inlet pressure be no less than 30 psi for all turbocharger models during normal operation (see p. 3.10 of the Garrett Overhaul Manual, TP20-0120-1).

After 30-psi (or more) oil enters the bearing area of the turbo, it mixes with air and emerges from the turbocharger with zero pressure, looking like dirty whipped cream. It is important that the drain line not only be larger than the inlet line, but have no flow restrictions in the return routing to the engine.

Semi-Floating Bearings

Floating bearings do a great job of dampening vibrations (and reducing associated wear) caused by rotor imbalance or external vibration. But it is actually the oil film, not the rotation of the bearing itself, that is responsible for the dampening. Hence it is possible to envision the use of a floating bearing that doesn't turn. This is precisely the scheme called out in Rajay Patent No. 3,043,636. In Rajay units, the bearing is kept from turning by a pin through a flange on one end of the bearing. This is known as a semi-floating bearing; it is used in all Rajay models.

One of the advantages of the semi-floating bearing design is that it doesn't centrifuge oil away from the shaft (an important consideration in a turbo turning at 100,000 rpm). It is thus possible to operate the turbocharger without damage at very low oil pressures. Rajay specifies 10 psi at idle, and 25 psi oil pressure in normal operation, but these figures are probably quite conservative. In an oil-pressure emergency, a Rajay turbo ought (all other things being equal) to outlast an AiResearch turbo by a considerable margin.

Bearing Housing

The bearing housing or center section (cartridge, in Rajay parlance) which holds the bearings and turbo shaft doesn't usually reach extremely high temperatures, but because floating bearings rotate at up to half of the shaft rpm, the housing must be of fairly hard material—usually cast iron. (Some turbos with full-floating bearings have been designed with aluminum center housings, but the design always called for a cast-iron sleeve in the bore, which adds to production cost.)

With semi-floating bearings (bearings that don't rotate), the hardness of the bearing housing is not critical, and it becomes possible to utilize an aluminum bearing housing. Such a housing offers definite advantages in terms of weight and ease of production. For these reasons, Rajay uses aluminum for its bearing housings.

Whether an aluminum bearing housing is really a good idea in terms of repairability is another matter. "When you tear into a Rajay at 1,000 hours," one turbo overhauler told us, "you almost always find that aluminum center section is shot. It's not a question of rebuild so

Most turbo systems incorporate a popoff valve or dump valve to protect against overboost. The object in the center of this photo is a dump valve for a TSIO-520-B Continental.

much as replacement." Of course, the good news is that replacement cartridges are cheap; in many cases, a Rajay can be rebuilt for a bit under $300.

Real-World TBOs

The turbos that work the hardest live the shortest lives, and in aviation the blowers that fit that category are generally Rajay models. Roto-Master chief engineer Hugh MacInnes, when he was alive, was fond of saying that "Small turbochargers are all basically simple, rugged devices and when treated properly will last as long as the engine." Real-world TBOs of 500 to 1,000 hours, however, are frequently mentioned by Rajay owners, who cite turbo housing cracking as a main cause of early retirement. (In 1981, Roto-Master switched to D2 Ni-resist in turbo housings, but this did not totally cure the housing cracking problem.) The Rajays that get the best life seem to be those that are coupled to manual wastegates and are infrequently used. The worst offenders are the fixed-wastegate ("can't turn 'em off") models used on Continental TSIO-360s and Enstrom helicopters.

AiResearch's tiny T04 seems to hold up as well or better than the best Rajays, and is more easily rebuilt, to boot. (Factory and PMA-built undersize bearings are available for all AiResearch models.) Unfortunately, it is not legal to replace a Rajay unit with an AiResearch component; getting approval, for example, to replace a Turbo Arrow's Rajay 325E101 with an AiResearch T04 would probably be difficult and costly. Why didn't Continental choose the T04 for the TSIO-360-F to begin with? According to one Continental engineer who was there at the time, "Garrett's T04 wasn't available then, so we had to go with Rajay."

The larger AiResearch turbos—the TE0659, TH08, and T18 series—seem to go to engine TBO with fair regularity, except perhaps in instances where the duty cycle is particularly severe (in which case the engine seldom makes its normal TBO, either). The widely used TE0659 has undergone numerous changes and improvements over the years (spelled out in Continental Service Bulletin M85-6 and Garrett Service Letter TP61-0001, Rev. E). There have been instances of compressor

The Rajay 325E-series turbocharger is used on the Aerostar 601, Piper Seneca II and III, Turbo Arrow, Mooney 231, Enstrom F-28A helicopter, and a wide range of aftermarket-STC'd retrofits. The gas outlet opening is only 2.6 inches across; turbine rotor is less than five inches in diameter.

rubbing and housing cracking in these turbos, but the full-floating bearing design—and generally low operating rpm—have resulted in these turbos achieving a good to very good service record. Overhaul can generally be accomplished for under $1,000; exchange for an OHC (overhauled/certified) unit runs $1,200 to $2,200 depending on model.

Overhaul Information

For information on Rajay overhaul or repair, contact Century Aircraft Corp. (Roto-Master's exclusive agent for G.A. sales), P.O. Box 31026, Amarillo, TX 79120 (phone 806/335-2806, Telex 738409 CEN-AIRCORP).

Remanufacturing of Rajay and AiResearch turbine shafts (including straightening, grinding, plating, balancing, and NDI) is now available through Southwest Aeroservice, FAA Repair Station 212-11, 422 S. St. Louis Ave., Tulsa, OK 74120 (918/587-4161). FAA-PMA replacement parts for many turbochargers, as well as quality repair and calibration services (not only for turbos but controllers and actuators) are available from Kel-Pak Industries, Inc., 1545 E. Acequia, Visalia, CA 93291 (209/627-3600).

For information on AiResearch turbochargers, Garrett now has a toll-free hotline: 1-800-421-2051 (Ext. 1949), or 213/517-1949. Or write Garrett at 3201 Lomita Blvd., Torrance, CA 90505.

WASTEGATES AND CONTROLLERS

Considering that there are only two turbocharger brands in aviation today—Rajay and AiResearch (Schwitzer almost made the list years ago, under the Alcor aegis)—it's only natural to assume that aircraft turbo sytems are lumpable into two neat categories, the only real question being whether to buy Brand 'R' or Brand 'A.' Not so. Aside from the fact that Rajays come only in small sizes (hence the use of double blowers on 540-Lycomings, for example, and big-block Chevrolets)—and aside from a few small technical details (e.g., Rajay's use of a semi-floating bearing)—there are no overwhelming hardware differences between Rajay and AiResearch. But there *are* a great many *installation* differences from airplane model to airplane model (even within a given turbo-P/N series), leading in turn to important differences in flyability and reliability.

The most important installation variable, arguably, is the choice of *controller*. All turbochargers are capable of producing more boost than an engine can stand. Conversely, all engines are capable of overdriving a turbocharger. (Explosion containment remains the primary consideration in turbo housing design.) Clearly, some means must be provided for regulating the turbocharger's output.

Manual Wastegates

Tweaking a turbocharger's output is, of course, done by opening of closing a trap door in the exhaust pipe called a *wastegate*. When the wastegate is closed, all engine exhaust, of necessity, goes through the turbine—or "exducer"—portion of the turbocharger. Open the wastegate, and all or most of the flow bypasses the exducer. (For this reason, engineers often eschew the term "wastegate" in favor of *bypass valve*.)

The question arises as to

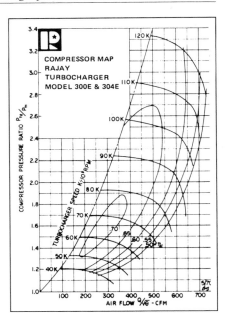

Flow map for the Rajay 300-series turbo shows that even at relatively modest pressure ratios (1.6 to 1.8), turbine speeds can easily exceed 70,000 rpm. At 18,000 feet, where outside air pressure is 15 inches, the turbo must operate at a pressure ratio of 2.0 to produce a cruise manifold pressure of 30 inches.

how to control the wastegate. In the interest of simplicity, you might well ask "Why not just rig the wastegate halfway-open, and leave it at that?" This approach is in fact used in the Continental TSIO-360-E/F/G series engines (in the Piper Seneca, Turbo Arrow, and Mooney 231). Unfortunately, it's not very efficient: You can't "turn off" the boost at sea level, and you can't *increase* the boost (i.e., close the wastegate all the way) at altitude, when you most need it. Typically, in this system, the power knobs are very sensitive (over-boosting is a real danger, despite protective relief valves); takeoff power, at sea level, is achieved at only 40 percent of throttle travel. What's more, the pilot must increase throttle as manifold pressure falls off in the climb (and reduce it as it picks up in the descent).

Fixed wastegates are a lousy compromise—kind of like safety-wiring the throttle half-open and attempting to modulate power with mixture. For maximum effective use of a turbocharger's capabilities, it only makes sense to be able to open and close the wastegate all the way. One of the simplest ways to do this is with manual (push/pull, Bowden-cable) wastegate controls—the so-called "second throttle" approach preferred by Rajay (and practiced extensively by

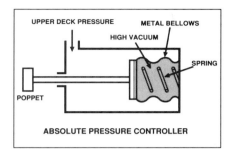

The absolute pressure controller is a simple aneroid spring-loaded to a poppet valve controlling oil flow to a hydraulic wastegate. The upper deck is kept at a constant absolute pressure.

Piper and Aero Commander in the early '60s). Here, you take off with wastegates open, climb normally, and—somewhere around 5,000 or 6,000 feet—start adding a little boost (one inch of manifold pressure per thousand feet) by turning the wastegate verniers, or flipping the WG switches (in Aerostars, and some Aztecs). Since the engine is never ground-boosted (except by mistake), this setup is known as *turbo-normalizing.*

WG-Throttle Interconnect

If you enjoy driving a stick shift, chances are you'd get along just fine with manual wastegates. Long cable runs create problems in twins, however (Bob Hoover's Shrike has manual Rajays, for instance, but the WG verniers seldom work); and there's always the danger of overboosting. All you need to do is forget the "wastegates open" part of the preflight checklist—just once—and you stand an excellent chance of converting your precious Continental or Lycoming into a $15,000 boat anchor filled with ashtrays.

A slight (very slight) improvement on the second-throttle approach is the "throttle-wastegate interconnect" scheme used in, among others, the Piper Turbo Saratoga and Rockwell 112TC. Here, the separate wastegate control is done away with by mechanically linking the throttle butterfly to the turbo wastegate. Which certainly *sounds* simple enough...but rigging (trust me) calls for a sense of humor, and throttle sensitivity is—how shall put it?—a real bitch. Once again, overboost is a concern; and constant fidgeting with power knobs during (and after) the climb is de rigueur.

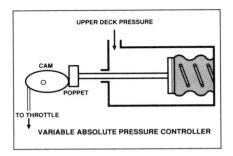

The variable absolute pressure controller has a throttle connection to limit aneroid action. Beech Duke is among the planes that use this type of controller.

Some of the "one knob" systems' sensitivity can be eliminated by designing the linkages in such a way that the first half of throttle travel opens the carburetor butterfly, while the last half closes the turbo wastegate. This is done in the Turbo Skylane, for example. But the other problems mentioned still apply. And one-knob systems tend to have considerable control friction, with interesting possibilities, also, for control creep, mechanical failure, and rigging drift caused by tolerance buildup in the linkages.

The Ideal System

The ideal system, you'll probably agree, is one in which: [1] there are no separate cockpit controls other than the throttle . . . [2] manifold pressure, once set, doesn't change during climb or descent. . . [3] over-boosting is impossible . . . and [4] mechanical complexity is minimized. (Actually, there are some people—Al Hundere of Alcor, certain bush pilots, ag operators, ex-military pilots—who would quibble with the third item, arguing that the ability to overboost in an emergency is actually a very valuable benefit of the manual systems. Keep this in mind when you go shopping for a T-plane.)

We come now to the automatic controllers. Imagine, if you will, putting a small aneroid in your engine's upper deck. ("Upper deck" refers to the intake system upstream of the throttle butterfly. Manifold pressure is taken *down-*

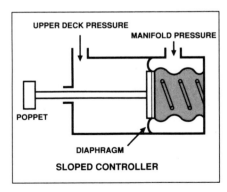

The sloped controller provides a set margin of extra pressure in the upper deck, over and above the manifold pressure commanded by the pilot. Late-model Turbo Centurions use this scheme.

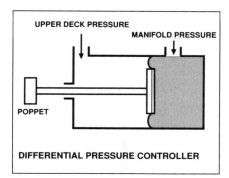

UPPER DECK PRESSURE

MANIFOLD PRESSURE

POPPET

DIFFERENTIAL PRESSURE CONTROLLER

Differential pressure controller references deck pressure against manifold pressure and keep the former about six inches higher than the latter. It is used in the Lycoming TIO-540-C1A, among others.

stream of the butterfly.) We will set the aneroid to 29.92 inches of mercury, say, so that at sea level on a standard day, the aneroid assumes its normal shape. Now obviously, if you were to take off and go to 1,000 feet, the aneroid would expand in response to the barometric change (since the pressure at 1,000 ft. is approximately one inch less than at sea level). At 2,000 feet, the aneroid will expand even more, since the pressure has fallen to about 27.92 inches. This, of course, is the principle upon which the barometric altimeter is based.

Suppose we use the aneroid's expansion, however, not to drive a meter movement (as in an altimeter), but to control a turbo wastegate. Suppose, in other words, we attach a small rod to the aneroid, which will travel back and forth in response to pressure (or altitude) changes; and suppose the rod, in turn, controls a servo motor or hydraulic actuator that opens and closes the wastegate. The net effect—if we rig everything correctly—is to create a *self-regulating* turbo system that seeks to maintain a *constant 29.92 inches of pressure in the upper deck.*

This is, in fact, the controller system used on the author's Turbo 310. It's called an *absolute pressure* controller, since the system seeks to maintain the upper deck at one, and only one absolute pressure. In my 310's case, the deck setpoint pressure happens to be 32.0 inches of mercury (which is also redline manifold pressure). *Downstream* of the throttle butterfly, of course, the manifold pressure is whatever you or I command with the throttle; the throttle buttefly functions to "leak" deck pressure, in the desired quantity, to the cylinders. Note, however, that there is *no mechanical connection whatsoever between throttle and controller.* The controller is autonomous—it has a mind of its own, like the thermostat on your home central heating system.

In construction, the absolute pressure controller—AiResearch P/N 470688—is almost as simple as an altimeter (and not that much more expensive, at $502 exchange). It consists of a metal bellows, vacuum-charged and spring-loaded, in a two-piece housing with oil inlet and

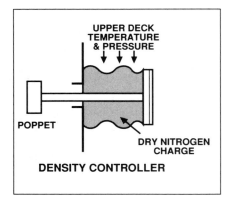

UPPER DECK
TEMPERATURE
& PRESSURE

POPPET

DRY NITROGEN
CHARGE

DENSITY CONTROLLER

The density controller compensates not only for pressure variations, but temperature variations as well (hence density). This type of controller limits peak output of Lycoming TIO-540-C1A at full throttle. (At partial throttle, differential pressure controller cuts in.

outlet holes (and of course a pressure sensing orifice). The bellows moves a poppet valve, which in turn controls oil pressure to the (hydraulically actuated) wastegate. (Engine oil is used for actuation in all automatic controller systems, at least in light aircraft.)

Most turbo systems using the absolute-pressure controller also incorporate a popoff-type overboost relief valve, but the controller itself, you'll notice, is a pretty good anti-overboost device (assuming it doesn't get hung up in the closed position)—and since the wastegate needs oil pressure to close, a plumbing failure results in *lack* of boost, rather than overboost. All in all, a rather simple—and safe—setup.

Sloped Controllers

Still, you might well ask why it's necessary to carry an absolute pressure of 32 inches (or whatever) in the upper deck at all times, when the acutal demand for manifold pressure might only be 25 inches, say, in cruise. Why not maintain the upper deck at manifold-pressure-plus-2.0 inches (or some similar margin)?

This is the rationale behind the so-called sloped *controller* (used, for example, on late-model Cessna P210 and T210 aircraft). The sloped controller is essentially an aboslute pressure controller with one added element: a diaphragm with one side referenced to the upper deck, and the other side plumbed to the lower deck (below the throttle). The controller "compares" the upper and lower decks, and tries to maintain a certain pressure excess above the throttle. In all other respects (plumbing, flyability), the sloped controller is identical to the plain-Jane absolute pressure controller described above.

The advantage of the sloped controller, of course, is that it reduces the part-throttle workload of the turbo. The disadvantage is slow acceleration (turbo lag) and possible surging.

Variable Absolute Pressure

Acutally, it's possible to achieve the "manifold-pressure-plus" performance curve of the sloped controller *without* added plumbing, reference ports, or diaphragms. All you need to do is make the absolute pressure controller's internal poppet valve (the oil outlfow valve) *externally adjustable* —and vary the adjustment with the throttle setting. This gives you, of course, a *variable absolute pressure controller* (used in the Beech Duke and Cessna Turbo Skymaster, to name two examples). It's one of few automatic controller schemes with a direct mechanical linkage to the throttle. What you have is an arm linking the throttle butterfly (at the fuel injector) to a cam at the controller; as the cam rotates, a tappetlike follower moves up or down, shifting the "closed" (setpoint) position of the oil-outflow poppet seat inside the controller. When the throttle is left alone, the controller behaves like an absolute pressure controller.

Density Controllers

There are still othe ways of doing things: The *differential pressure controller* (favored by Piper for the Navajos and Turbo Aztecs) uses a pressure-comparison diaphragm with one side referenced to the upper deck and the other side referenced downstream of the throttle—the idea being, once again, for the controller to maintain a certain pressure excess above the throttle plate at all times (in this case, a fairly hefty 6.0 inches or so). Unlike the sloped controller, however, the differential pressure controller has no absolute-pressure-reference aneroid (which means it can't automatically correct for changes in altitude). In engines with this system, Lycoming always places a *density controller* in the control loop as well, to take over at high manifold pressure (i.e., 90 percent power or better). The two controllers work in concert to prevent overboosts, and for this reason no separate relief valve is used on engines that employ this setup (Lycoming TIO-360-A; TIO-540-A, C, F, J and N).

The density controller is an unusual device. Instead of using a spring-loaded, vacuum-containing aneroid (which can sense only pressure—not temperature), the density controller uses a nitrogen-charged aneroid which "sits in the breeze" in the upper deck, sensing both temperature *and* pressure (hence density). The density controller should, theoretically, correct for density altitude. And it does. As a result, on a plane with density controllers, you never know—from day to day—exactly how much manifold pressure the controllers are going to give you on takeoff. The controllers on a Navajo Chieftain, for example, are adjusted to give 44.0 inches of manifold pressure on takeoff, on a standard day at sea level. But on a 100-degree day, full throttle may yield 47.0 inches (redline is 49 inches). Conversely, on a cold day, you may not be able to get more than 42.5 inches. (What's worse, each of the plane's two engines may react somewhat differently to the change in conditions.) All of this is normal—for a Navajo.

Density controller systems are reliable. But their Rube Goldberg-like plumbing and high parts counts render overhauls expensive, and routine adjustments tend to be time-consuming. In terms of flyability, the density system rates—at best—only fair. Why Piper (or anybody) would choose this sytem from among the simpler alternatives available is, frankly, hard to imagine. Maybe the Devil made them do it.

Rate Controllers

Not that the pressure-reference systems are without pitfalls; some have so much built-in hysteresis, or are so sensitive to throttle-jockeying, that some form of surge protection is called for. This need is addressed by the *rate controller,* a simple device which is sometimes used in tandem with the absolute pressure controller (as on the early Turbo Skymaster) or the variable absolute pressure controller (as on the Cessna 411 and 401). The rate controller adds one more diaphragm to the system—but here, *both* sides of the diaphragm are plumbed to the upper deck, with one side sensing pressure through a tiny restrictor orifice (and the other through a larger port), so that the diaphragm only moves if there's a sudden rush of pressure. Clever, these Americans.)

Some engines are capable of driving their turbochargers to destructive speeds under high-power, high-altitude (thin air), closed-wastegate conditions, in which case a means must be provided for keeping the turbocharger in one piece (i.e., slowing it down). The usual solution is a *pressure ratio* controller, which may be built into the absolute pressure controller (Turbo 310) or added on as a separate unit (Cessna 401, 320D). "Pressure ratio" is a common turbo engineering term—it refers to the ratio of compressor discharge to ambient (inlet) air pressure. (Turbine rpm is proportional to the outlet/inlet pressure ratio.) Not unexpectedly, a pressure ratio controller contians a diaphragm (and oil-metering poppet) referenced to the inlet and outlet sides of the turbo compressor. Simple.

One thing all automatic controller systems have in common, since wastegate actuation occurs via engine oil pressure, is a tendency to work sluggishly in cold weather. For this reason, some caution must be exercised with the throttles on the first takeoff of the day, in winter conditions. Generally, if you wait until the oil-temperature needle has come off the peg, you'll be safe. (It helps to use multiviscosity oil, too.)

INTERCOOLING

Intercooling is a wonderful innovation (if anything 50 years old can be called an "innovation"), but it's important to understand what it can and cannot do. It's not the panacea some people think it is.

An intercooler, of course, is nothing more than a radiator—a device for rejecting heat. You pump hot air through it and it comes out cold. (Not really cold; just less hot.) Obviously, the more heat you've got to get rid of in the first place, the more you stand to enjoy whatever benefits there are to be enjoyed through intercooling.

Trying to cool air with air isn't easy, however. Find the difference in air temperature at the hot and cold ends of the intercooler, divide that by the difference between CDT and OAT (compressor discharge temp and outside air temp), multiply by 100, and you've got the intercooler's efficiency in percent. This number generally works out to around 50 percent. If someone tell you their intercooler is 90 percent efficient, they're lying. If they tell you 40 percent, they're probably not jiving, and you should ask yourself whether the benefits of such minimal cooling are worth it, for your type of flying.

What are the benefits? Chiefly the ability to get more power at a given manifold pressure (and do it with better detonation margin). Intercooled air is cooler and denser. The effect is just like shutting off the carburetor heat. Depending on how much heat there was to begin with, the effect can be attention-getting, or (then again) not too impressive.

For example, if you have a plane with an inefficient turbo system (Mooney 231, Turbo Arrow, Seneca II/III, Turbo Saratoga) and you regularly fly to FL 180 or above, even a moderately effective intercooler will cut your CDTs by 100 degrees or more. Instead of 75-percent power being 30 inches and 2,600 rpm, say, it might be 26.5 inches and 2,600 rpm. (Intercooler kits come with revised power charts which become part of the airplane's Approved Flight Manual.) You've effectively lowered the density altitude.

On the other hand, if your plane has a relatively efficient turbo

Piper Turbo Arrow's TSIO-360-FB engine is one that benefits greatly from intercooling. The Continental engine's fixed-wastegate turbo system results in high compressor discharge temperatures nearly all the time. Intercooling lowers CDTs substantially, improving overall performance.

system, your CHTs are low, and you rarely fly above 10,000 feet, an intercooler isn't going to do much for you. (You probably don't need a turbocharger, either.)

Where the intercooler salespeople really get worked up is in the area of engine longevity. Intercooling gives lower CHTs, lower EGT and TIT (we're told), which can lead in turn to longer TBOs. Actually, the effect on CHT can be substantial, and if you were operating at or near detonation limits before, intercooling just may extend the life of your engine. But a one-degree drop in intake-air temperature does not give you a one-degree drop in EGT/TIT. Nor should you expect it to. Cooling the intake charge a few degrees before engulfing it in a powerful conflagration is (as Dave Noland would say) like throwing an ice cube in a heated swimming pool. The effect is hardly dramatic.

Aviation gasoline, by industry spec (ASTM D910), has a minimum heat content of 18,720 Btu per pound. Thus, a TSIO-520 engine burning 18 gallons (108 pounds) of fuel an hour is flowing around 2,021,760 Btu per hour, or 33,700 Btu per minute—about 5 Btu per combustion event.

At 2,400 rpm, and assuming 100 percent volumetric efficiency (which is easily possible in a turbocharged engine), a TSIO-520 is gulping 361 cubic feet of air per minute. That's something like 27 pounds of air per minute (give or take a couple pounds)—about 15 times as much air as fuel.

We're putting two forms of heat into the combustion chamber. One is heat from compression of the intake air by the turbocharger. Another is heat from combustion of fuel. The question is: How important is the former relative to the latter?

To answer that, suppose an intercooler drops our intake air temperature by 100 degrees Fahrenheit. Allowing for the specific heat of air (0.24), and assuming a 27 lb/min flow rate of air into the engine, we can calculate a 648-Btu difference between a minute's worth of air going in with intercooling versus without intercooling. In the non-intercooled engine, this 648 Btu combines with 33,700 Btu from 1.8 pounds of fuel (which we assume will burn completely—stoichiometrically) for a total of 34,348 "added" Btu in the combustion chamber. Get out your pocket calculator and you'll find that 648 is less than two percent of 34,348.

What does this mean? Well, the difference in temperature between the air going into a TSIO-520 (OAT) and the exhaust coming out (TIT) is about 1,500 degrees Fahrenheit. With intercooling, we can expect a reduction of this delta-T on the order of two percent—i.e., 30 degrees Fahrenheit.

Of course, there are many assumptions in this example. We neglect cooling of the intake air by fuel evaporation, for example, along with various heat losses ahead of the EGT probe, etc. But to a first approximation, at least, it's clear that a one-degree drop in intake-air temperature does not give you a one-degree drop in EGT or TIT. It gives you, at best, a few tenths of a degree drop in EGT.

So if you buy an intercooler (and you probably should, if you fly one of the planes mentioned earlier), don't expect to see vast reductions in EGT. (You won't.) Don't expect big reductions in cooling drag, either (radiators produce lots of drag). And don't expect to go faster (your engine's horsepower rating hasn't changed).

If you do buy intercooling, do it for the ability to obtain cruise power at a few inches less manifold pressure; do it for the improved critical altitude, the somewhat lower CHT, and the extra detonation margin. You'll save a few percent on fuel, too (the exact amount depending on how hot-running your engine was to begin with).

But forget about doubling your TBO. It's not going to happen.

SHUTDOWN

The period from touchdown to shutdown is a critical one for many engines, yet it is seldom discussed in Pilots' Operating Handbooks.

Reading most POHs, one gets the impression that once the plane is safely on the ground, shutdown is a simple matter of retarding the mixture and putting the keys in your hip pocket.

Not so. Turbocharged engines, for example, need a cooldown/ spooldown period of from four to eight minutes (running at idle on the ground) before the engine can safely be shut down; otherwise, heat soakback from the turbo will cause scorching (coking) of oil on the turbine shaft. After repeated hot shutdowns, coking will reach a point where—eventually—the turbo will no longer turn. Running the engine for four to eight minutes on the ground keeps oil flowing through the turbo bearings and gives the turbo a chance to cool down gradually. Usually by the time the CHT (cylinder head temp) gauge has registered a drop of 50 degrees or so, the engine can safely be stopped without the oil in the turbo coking up.

A brief cooldown period is advisable for *all* engines—not just turbocharged ones. Idling into the wind allows circulating oil to carry heat away from the upper cylinder head (rocker box) area. Also, as stated in Lycoming Service Instruction No. 1425, "Shutting the engine down before it has sufficiently cooled down can induce valve sticking." Again, a useful rule of thumb is to consider the engine ready for shutdown when CHT has dropped 50 degrees, or to where it shows no sign of going any lower.

Owners of fuel-injected engines need to pay special attention to power management after touchdown. A special Maintenance Tips bulletin by RAM Aircraft Corp. (dated 11/85) has the following to say:

"At reduced power settings, as during descent, approach, and landing, the fuel flow per horsepower ratio increases. The rich mixture manifests itself as a lot of cold fuel entering a hot cylinder intake air port at the fuel injection nozzle outlet. The conditions for 'shock' cooling have [thus] been met—rapid an uneven cooling which can cause a crack between the fuel injection nozzle and spark plug hole."

Corrective action? "Correction action is to lean the mixture during descent and landing (1,300 F to 1,400 F on the RAM range-marked, temperature calibrated EGT should do) and do not enrichen the mixture until on the runway with throttles at idle."

In other words, RAM believes (based on their repeated finding of cracks in cylinder head between the injector nozzle and top spark plug) that the widespread practice of ramming the mixture knob to full rich before landing has the effect of shock-cooling the intake port area, with consequent crack formation.

This is a good reason to make sure injector nozzle air ports and screens are free of debris that could interfere with atomization of fuel. All injector nozzles (whether Bendix/Lycoming or Continental) have a side-orifice through which air is drawn for atomization of the spray. In normal operation, no atomization occurs at high manifold pressure, since a delta-P of 10 inches Hg or more is required to cause air to be sucked in through the side-hole. Atomization thus occurs mainly at idle, when manifold pressure is at 12 inches or so (and ambient pressure outside the nozzle is 29 or 30 inches). If the nozzle is dirty, however, atomization may be impaired, in which case a steady stream of fuel (the size of a pencil lead) is directed at a small spot on the cylinder's intake port. After a long flight, this fuel is likely to be quite cold (from cold-soaking at altitude), particularly in a turbocharged aircraft. Obviously, pointing a steady, defined stream of zero-degree liquid at a hot piece of cast aluminum is not a good idea, if you want to avoid cracking.

The answer is to clean your injector nozzles on a regular schedule— say every 100 hours—and avoid enrichening the mixture until you have turned off the main runway and are taxiing back to the tiedown spot. (Obviously you should enrichen for a go-around, if need be. Use common sense.)

A lean shutdown pays dividends in terms of plug fouling (and easy

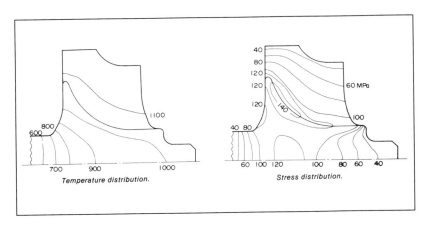

Temperature and stress distributions on turbocharger turbine blades give an indication of how hostile the turbocharger's operating environment is. Heat soakback to the rotor shaft after shutdown is a potentially serious problem since it can cause coking of the oil.

starting), too: Try running the engine at 1,200 rpm, leaned to very nearly the point of misfire, for 30 seconds just before shutdown (after your four to eight-minute cooling off period). Then bring the throttle back to the idle stop, and retard the mixture to idle cutoff. The 1,200-rpm leanout causes spark plug core temperatures to rise to the point where carbon, oil, and lead deposits are vaporized, so that plugs remain clean during shutdown. At the next startup, less cranking will be required since all plugs will be in good working order.

If your plane has a boost pump, be sure to turn it off before shutting the engine down with the mixture; many engines will tend to "run on" (false dieseling) if the electric fuel pump is operating as shutdown is attempted. Of course, with the boost pump off and the mixture in ICO (idle cutoff), if the engine wants to continue to run, you could well have an internally leaking carburetor or fuel injector (or primer). Get it checked out.

In aircraft with Bendix pressure carburetors, it's a good idea to return the mixture control to the mid-travel point after engine shutdown. This prevents diaphragms in the carburetor from taking a set and affecting fuel-flow on the next flight.

Whatever you do, *don't* turn the fuel selector off between flights (unless serious fuel-system maintenance is to be performed). It's too easy to forget to turn it back on.

Chapter 5

PROPELLER GOVERNORS

Few aviation companies are older than the Wright Brothers, but aviation's oldest prop-governor company—Woodward Governor of Rockford, Illinois—can legitimately make that claim. Woodward originally made governors for water wheels (and continues to supply governors for a variety of non-aviation-related applications today). But when Amos Woodward patented his first governor design around 1870, the concept of using centrifugal flyweight action to control an engine's rpm was already 100 years old, having been employed by James Watt in the first steam engines. So in a sense it can be said that the prop governor is one of the oldest, most primitive parts of an airplane's anatomy—the lizard brain of the modern Bonanza.

Aircraft governors don't use massive iron balls for flyweights, but—small technical details aside—today's Woodward governors operate on much the same principle as any steam-engine governor of

days gone by, or for that matter, any contemporary Hartzell or McCauley governor. (A few Skylanes had Garwin governors, but most have since been converted to Wooward 210065 or McCauley C290D2/T1 governors, for which parts are widely available.) Open any of these units up, and you'll see the same basic parts, performing the same basic functions.

The unit we chose to dissect and photograph for this chapter is a Woodward Type CSSA, Model A210680 governor from a G33 Bonanza. One reason we chose it is that the Type CSSA (Constant-Speed, Single-Acting) Woodward governor is probably the most numerous single-engine (non-feathering-prop) governor in the fleet, and is typical—in construction, mounting, service needs, and TBO life—of the vast majority of General Aviation governors, regardless of name-brand. Another reason we chose it is that this particular unit was leaking oil like a sieve (a pressurized sieve). It desperately needed to come off for service.

Technically speaking, of course, prop governor maintenance is not something the pilot can legally do himself. It is also not something the *A&P mechanic* can do legally. If anything more than gasket replacement or minor rig adjustments are needed, your A&P is legally bound to send the governor off for repair by a certificated repair station. Your mechanic cannot repair governors legally. He can only remove and install replacements governors. Which is why the first thing a mechanic is likely to do if you come into the shop complaining of "governor problems" is take your governor off and give it to the UPS man and tell you to come back in two weeks with $275.

However, many governor problems aren't. So before consigning yourself to the ranks of the AOG (Aircraft Owners on the Ground), do a little troubleshooting; gain some familiarity with failure modes, trouble clues, remedies and contraindications. If your problem *does* turn out to reside in the governor, you can pull the unit yourself when the time comes, and save a few bucks on removal—and (with a logbook signoff from an A&P) you can even put the yellow-tagged (overhauled and certified) replacement in yourself.

Theory of Governor Operation

The term "constant-speed prop" is something of a misnomer, if you think about it, since the C/S feature of any "constant-speed propeller" is not in the prop but the governor (and in any case, the rpm is seldom perfectly constant). There was a time when high-performance air-

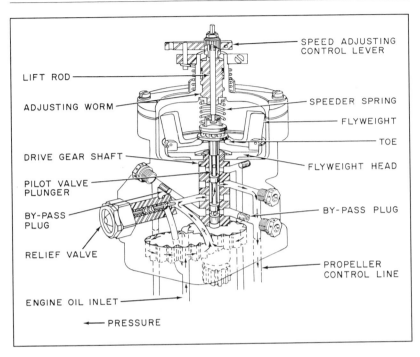

Major components of the Woodward CSSA (constant-speed, single-acting) propeller governor.

planes had controllable-speed props with manual cockpit control over blade pitch. The pilot would set the pitch for cruise, or for climb, or whatever, as needed to keep the engine in the right rpm range. Unfortunately, this was a less than satisfactory arrangement, because rpm varied unrelentingly with each up and downdraft, each change in air pressure, each change in pitch, etc. The slightest airspeed or attitude change would result in a wild rpm excursion (or at least an annoying rpm change). With manual pitch control, the prop behaved essentially as a fixed-pitch prop any time the pilot let go of the prop-pitch control. What pilots needed—especially pilots of multiengine airplanes, like the Stinson and Ford Trimotors (whose engines were *never* in sync)—was an "autopilot" just for the control of engine rpm. Preferably one that would also give the pilot control, indirectly, over prop pitch as well.

The modern prop governor (insofar as any governor can be called "modern") frees the pilot of the burden of moment-to-moment rpm

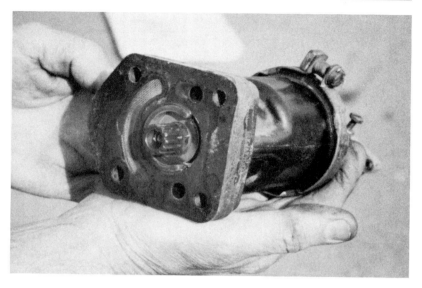

Woodward governor as removed from Bonanza's IO-470-N engine. Notice the fine-mesh oil screen built into the mounting gasket.

management while nevertheless allowing adjustments to be made in the "final drive ratio" of the engine. With a constant-speed prop, the pilot can (in effect) "downshift" when going uphill. You don't actually downshift, of course, but you select a higher rpm—a lower blade pitch—when climbing, which results in more revolutions of the crankshaft per unit of forward travel. Which is what most of us mean by downshifting.

But you'll notice there is a big difference between constant-speed (governed) prop action and manually controllable pitch. When you set your prop governor for, say, 2,500 rpm at sea level (during initial climbout), it will still be 2,500 rpm at 10,000 feet; yet the air is much thinner at 10,000 feet than at sea level. If you're flying a Turbo Centurion and can maintain climb power all the way up, the only way rpm can remain constant during the climb is if blade pitch increases as the air gets thinner. (Otherwise, the engine would overspeed.) Setting rpm is one thing; setting blade pitch is another. When you set rpm on a governed prop, you're not setting blade pitch—the blade pitch will vary with IAS (indicated airspeed, which in turn varies with air density) and engine torque.

From a mechanical standpoint, the main thing to know about a prop governor is that it is basically nothing more than an oil pump whose output is regulated by a flyweight system. The governor takes engine oil from a crankcase gallery (already flowing at 50 or 60 psi of pressure) and boost it to as much as 200 psi of pressure before diverting it to the prop dome, where there is a sliding piston attached to pitch links that control the pitch of your propeller blades. When oil pressure presses on the piston, the blades change pitch in proportion to the pressure applied.

The governors in use on light aircraft are of the "single-acting" type, which means that oil pressure is supplied to actuate the prop blades in one direction only. In most aircraft, oil pressure is used to move the blades to low pitch (high rpm). Counterweights on the blades, in conjunction with springs and/or aerodynamic forces, tend to oppose the changes wrought by oil pressure. In other words, counterweight action tends to place the prop blades in high pitch, while oil pressure is used to effect low pitch (or in some cases, vice versa). Oil pressure is *not* used to move the blades into high *as well as* low pitch. (That would be a *double-acting* governor system.)

For now, it's enough to remember that the prop governor is an integral part of your engine's oil system. It uses engine oil to effect changes in prop (engine) rpm. Like any other part of your engine oil system, the prop governor depends—for its longevity and proper functioning—on an adequate supply of clean oil of the proper viscosity. *Congealed oil, sludgy or dirty oil, thinned (overheated) oil, all have an effect on prop governor action.* (The governor is an oil pump, and can cavitate under adverse conditions just like any oil pump.) You can't expect to supply a governor contaminated, congealed, or overheated oil and wind up with good rpm control.

Speed Up, Slow Down

If you pull a governor off of its AND20010 drive pad—which can either be at the front of the engine (ahead and below the number-six jug on a Continental), or at the rear of the engine, on the accessory case (for some Lycomings and older Continentals)—you'll see that at the base of the unit is a gear-type oil pump very similar in design to the main oil pump in your engine. (The gears—one "drive" gear, one "idler" gear—have 12 teeth and run at crankshaft rpm in Continentals, or at from 0.866 to 1.3 times crankshaft rpm in Lycomings, depending on exact engine model.) These gears provide the oil pressure needed for prop actuation.

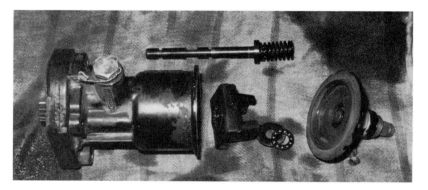

With the end cap removed, the flyweight ball-bearing assembly, flyweights, speeder spring, and shaft come out easily.

Inside the governor body, various oil channels allow high-pressure oil to flow either to the prop dome or back to the crankcase. (If oil pressure should get dangerously high—due to an obstruction in a passageway, for example—a spring-loaded relief valve will dump excess oil back to the engine.) Metering of pressurized oil to the prop dome occurs by *pilot valve* action. The pilot valve is nothing but a plunger turning with the main governor drive shaft whose vertical movements control oil "leakage" to the prop hub. The vertical movements of the pilot valve plunger are, of course, controlled by L-shaped flyweights bearing against the mushroomed end of the plunger. The flyweights pivot at the bend in the 'L,' the small ends of the weights bearing (in turn) against spring pressure. The spring that tends to dampen up and down movement of the pilot valve is called the *speeder spring*. The balance of flyweight pressure against speeder spring pressure determines the setpoint position (or on-speed position) of the pilot valve.

In the Cockpit

On the outside of the governor is a control arm which connects (via rods and cables) to the prop lever in the cockpit. Movement of this pivoting control arm causes tension to be increased or decreased on the speeder spring inside the top of the governor. This results in the pilot valve seeking a new setpoint (on-speed) position.

Any subsequent overspeed or underspeed of the engine will cause the flyweights to pull or push on the pilot valve in such a manner that the pilot valve shifts just the right amount to cause the prop to slow down or speed up just enough to return the engine to its original "setpoint" rpm.

To recapitulate: The prop governor is an externally mounted oil pump that selectively "leaks" oil pressure (at anywhere from 50 to 200 psi, as needed) to the prop hub, where it is converted to piston motion and blade pitch changes. Precise metering of oil pressure occurs by action of a plunger-type valve inside the hollow drive shaft of the governor, which (by moving up or down) covers or uncovers oil channels leading to the oil outlet ports of the governor, thence to the prop dome (via the crankshaft oil transfer collar). Centrifugal flyweight action tends to maintain the pilot valve at any given position. But the ultimate setpoint position of the pilot valve is determined from the cockpit, by the action of the pilot, who—by pushing or pulling on a cable—loads or unloads the speeder spring (which bears against the toes of the L-shaped flyweights).

Troubleshooting

"Since governor action is directly related to the propeller pitch changing mechanism," notes the anonymous author of Woodward's CSSA *Maintenance Handbook* (Bulletin No. 33001B), "there are very few governor troubles that can be isolated with the governor installed and operating. Failure of the propeller to change pitch correctly might be caused either by the governor or propeller. [Therefore] except for locating obvious troubles, it is best to replace the governor with one known to be in good condition when trouble occurs in the propeller pitch-changing system." It takes an exceptionally canny operator, in many cases, to pinpoint the governor itself as the true source of an rpm-related problem. So don't feel bad if after trying all of the tricks discussed in this chapter, you *still* end up having to remove the governor and replace it with a different one. This is still the best method for isolating a governor problem to the governor.

While we're dispensing caveats, let's also stop to point out that as engine accessories go, prop governors are devilishly reliable. If vacuum pumps were half as reliable as prop governors, the people who sell standby vacuum systems would be on Food Stamps and product liability lawyers might be forced to find meaningful employment.

Another caveat that might be appropriate to mention at this time is that a disproportionate number of governor "malfunctions" occur immediately after prop or governor maintenance. Return to service after a prop overhaul or engine major overhaul is often when governor problems first show up.

One of the most common "governor" complaints is failure of the prop rpm to stabilize in flight ("hunting" of the prop). This can be due to sludge in the governor; a sticky pilot valve; or high leakage in the oil transfer collar bearing at the front of the crankshaft. But by far the most common reason for prop "hunting" is excessive blade friction in the propeller. (In all likelihood, the prop is also slow to cycle in the morning—even with hot oil.) The thing to do is have an experienced prop man put a pair of blade paddles on the propeller and manually work the blades to determine whether friction is excessive. If the blades do not turn smoothly through their range of travel on the ground (with paddles on), you know that blade friction is to blame.

Hartzell owners should remove zerk fittings from the prop hub for the "paddle test," and regrease the prop hub at the end of the test and every 100 hours thereafter. Many Hartzell owners aren't aware that their props have grease fittings that need fresh grease periodically. (The approved procedure is to remove one fitting and force grease into the opposite fitting until fresh grease appears at the fittingless side.)

Non-Hartzell propellers do not have grease fittings in the hub. The blade pitch-change mechanisms get grease only at overhaul in such props.

If blade friction is normal, perform this simple test: Go up to altitude, and—once trimmed for level cruise—push the nose over into a dive without altering any power settings. When you've picked up 10 or 20 knots, check the rpm again; if the governor is governing, it won't have changed. On the other hand, if the prop rpm has gone up with airspeed, the governor isn't governing.

Sludge

Another perpetual problem with constant-speed props and governors is sludge buildup. The prop dome and crankshaft (and to a lesser degree, the hollow drive shaft of the governor itself) make pretty good centrifuges, and any particles much bigger than aphid dandruff are going to get permanently deposited (centrifuged out) on the inside diameter of the spinning shaft or dome. In particular, the oil-return hole in the end of the crankshaft is a fine place for soft-carbon sludge to accumulate. If you check your airplane service manual carefully, you'll probably find this mentioned as a 250-hour or 500-hour inspection point. In the days before ashless dispersant oil, it was quite

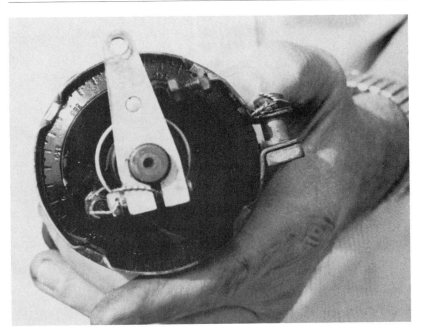

The rotational orientation of the end cap to the governor body (maintained by the circumferential clamp) is critical to proper governor operation.

common to remove propellers every 100 to 200 hours to desludge the crankshaft. (This is still S.O.P. in branches of the military that operate small piston aircraft.)

A typical first indication of trouble is difficulty getting the prop to cycle on runup. The owner complains of having to wait 10 or 20 seconds for the rpm to sag after pulling the prop control back, even with warm oil. A knowledgeable mechanic will want to know how long it's been since the prop has been off, what kind of oil is being used, and how often the oil and filters are changed. The owner might say he uses the plane only for short flights, changes the oil every 60 to 70 hours, and the plane has no filter. (Don't laugh; many, many C/S-prop aircraft have no oil filter—including the Bonanza from which we removed the Woodward governor shown in the accompanying photos.) The mechanic removes the guy's propeller, and lo! The crankshaft is plugged solid with soft sludge.

"I had this happen with my Bonanza," a former V35 owner of our acquaintance once admitted. "Prop action had gotten very slow over the course of several hundred hours. Pretty soon it got so bad, I couldn't do a decent deep-cycle on the ground. You should have seen my face when the A&P took the prop off and we saw what the oil return hole in the crankshaft looked like! Hell, you couldn't have stuck a piece of safety wire in the open part of the sludgy thing! It was damn near packed solid. It's a wonder I had any prop action at all."

The oil passage in the crankshaft can be cleaned out without further engine disassembly; however, getting sludge out of a prop dome or governor is another matter. If you can see sludge on the governor base pad gasket (after loosening the hold-down studs and pulling the governor away), it may be that all you need is a fresh gasket. The gasket used on most governors is a special type of custom gasket incorporating a fine-mesh metal screen, especially to keep sludge, dirt, feathers, Teflon scum, etc., out of the governor. When this screen gets covered over, governing action suffers—and you buy another gasket. (And maybe, you stop using oil additives.) Most pilots don't even know this screen exists.

Other Troubles

We've already covered the most common prop and governor difficulties: namely, failure of prop rpm to stabilize ("hunting," which can be caused by sludgy governor, high leakage rate in oil transfer bearing around crankshaft, sticky pilot valve, or high blade friction) and slow prop action (failure to cycle properly on the runup, usually caused by sludge in the system). If you live long enough, you're apt to come across several other types of governor mischief as well:

Minimum governing rpm set too high: This is where the prop's adjustable rpm range is narrower than it should be, and rpm droops prematurely when throttle is retarded. The culprit is incorrect rigging of the governor's *idle limit*, which is the upper portion of control shaft to which the control arm attaches at the governor. This rod bears directly on the speeder spring seat and thus (depending on how high or low it is set during final assembly of the governor at overhaul) can affect the "coming in" speed of the governor. Setting the height of this rod is somewhat analogous to setting the float height in a carburetor. Normally it is not adjusted in the middle of a TBO run.

Failure to feather: This can result from setting the lift rod (see above) too far the wrong direction at overhaul. If a newly installed governor fails to feather on command (and it's best to find this out ASAP after installing it, rather than wait until you have an actual engine failure), call the shop that overhauled the governor and ask them whether the person that overhauled your governor wasn't using the lift-rod settings for a *single-engine* installation rather than a twin.

Newly installed governor fails to change rpm: Newly installed governors often fail to govern, even if the part number and model number are correct. This is because the same model of governor can be used in either rotation (clockwise on some engines, counter- on others), depending on how the oil inlet holes in the base of the governor are plugged. Generally there are four holes requiring two plugs. In a Woodward governor, the holes marked 'A' are to be plugged off if the governor drive shaft is to be driven clockwise (as viewed head-on with the governor spline-end toward you, in your hand). If you're not sure which way the drive shaft is supposed to turn,

Speeder spring and flyweight assembly fits neatly in the palm of one hand.

of course, you should turn your prop through by hand while visually noting the direction of drive socket rotation in the AND 20010 pad on the engine.

Note: Some governors also incorporate bypass plugs in internal oil passages to control the direction of flow, and these plugs can get mixed up during overhaul, also resulting in failure to govern.

Oil Leaks

And then there are oil leaks—a good thing to watch for in any device operating under 200 psi of oil pressure. Because of the pressures involved, governor oil leaks tend to be messy indeed. Diagnosing a leaky governor is often a simple matter of slipping on an oil slick during the windshield-wipedown part of your usual walkaround inspection.

If you have to, clean the governor area with Gunk or Varsol, then run the engine and shut down, in order to isolate the source of the leak. Look closely at the base of the governor to distinguish gasket leaks (seen as oil coming from the parting line between base and gasket) from flange leaks (seen as oil coming from governor body to base junction). If you look at the Woodward governor in the accompanying photos, you'll notice that the base pad or flange is detachable. Working away from the crankcase, you have a gasket, a half-inch-thick base pad, the governor body, then the governor cover assembly (or top plate, containing the lift rod, control arm, and adjusting worm). Oil can leak from any of these places.

A gasket leak can, of course, usually be cured by simply installing a new MS 100009 gasket (see below for removal instructions). Sometimes all that's needed is to bring the mounting nuts up to proper torque (20 ft-lbs, or as specified in your service manual). Be sure all surfaces are smooth and clean before torquing things in place. Do *not* try to fix a gasket leak by *overtorquing* hold-down bolts. Torque to book values and no further.

If oil is coming out of the body/base-flange line, again, the cure is easy. Take the governor off, secure the base in a vise, remove the two fillister-head screws in the base at one and seven o'clock (relative to the relief valve at high noon), then lightly tap the drive gear with a plastic hammer to force the base off the body dowels. (Go slowly; tap lightly; and do not let loose parts fall on the ground.) *Do not* pry the base off with a sharp instrument which might damage the face of the metal.

You'll notice, when you've separated the base from the governor body, that there is a peculiar, semi-trapezoidal rubber seal in a groove in the base. Replace this seal with a new one (coat it lightly with clean oil), and if nicks or scratches in the metal around the seal are present, lap the parting faces of the base and body with fine abrasive cloth on a good surface plate as necessary. Do not attempt to interchange the base of one governor with the base or body of another of the same type, as differences in the alignment of the dowels in various base/body combinations will be enough to cause problems. (You can order a new base from the factory, but the base and body will have to be rereamed for oversize dowels, a procedure calling for special tools. This is best done by a repair shop.)

The Woodward governor in our photos was throwing oil not from the base or gasket, but from the control-arm end, where the lift rod exits the cover. There is an O-ring at the distal (most outboard) end of the lift-rod/actuator-worm bushing, and in our governor, this O-ring had failed. Unfortunately, getting the lift rod, etc., out in order to service the O-ring calls for special tools (i.e., one WT-19201 Lift Rod Extractor), and we were not able to service the unit ourselves. The cover was sent out to Santa Monica Propeller Service, Inc. (3025 Airport Ave., Santa Monica, CA 90405; phone 213/587-5363) for the necessary repair.

We were told, incidentally, that while fairly rare, rapid wear does sometimes occur in the worm actuator area at the top of the governor if there is excessive cable tension in the actuator cable going to the governor. (This puts an undue side load on the lift rod assembly, as you can well imagine.) The thing to do is check periodically to see that pivot points are lubed, pulleys free, and cable clamps sound, so that friction or tension doesn't build up in the cable run. (If you follow the cable from firewall to governor, particularly on a Bonanza or 182 or other airplane with forward-mounted governor, you'll be surprised how many cable support brackets there are. These brackets often fatigue-fail in service, due to cable and engine vibration. They should be checked every 100 hours or whenever the cowling is off.)

Catastrophic Failures

Catastrophic governor failures are rare, but relief valve springs do break, debris (from other parts of the engine) can hang up on pilot valves, O-rings blow out, and, of course, actuation cables do separate now and then. Also, actuator arms have been known to slip off governors at the lift rod, when inadequately safetied. The last time this happened to us was in a rented Skylane. Fortunately, we made a safe precautionary landing and no harm was done. Since then, we've become more careful to check governor connections on walkaround.

A C35 Bonanza pilot of our acquaintance was not quite as lucky. On the first flight after governor maintenance, the actuator-arm connection came loose on this man's governor about 500 feet off the departure end of runway 19 at El Monte, California (which is surrounded by industry, cars, and stucco). The propeller went to high pitch (low rpm) and the owner elected to perform a downwind landing, which was successful, except that in running off the north end of the runway a drainage gulley was hit, wiping out the Bonanza's nose gear. An entire nose section had to be ordered from Beech, and the owner was more than 10 months getting back into the air. (The insurance company, interestingly, paid all the repair bills but refused the owner's request to convert from Goodyear to Cleveland brakes.)

The moral of these stories is that when a governor malfunctions in

Base plate removed, the governor's oil-pump gears are clearly visible. (Note the specially shaped oil-seal gasket.) The impellers of the governor are capable of stepping up crankcase oil pressure two to three times, for prop actuation.

a big way (and this is true of internal failures as well as cable failures), the result is often a significant power loss. Should a governor's oil-pump gears crunch up, for example, all oil pressure to the prop dome will be lost and the prop blades will (on most aircraft) automatically seek high pitch, through counterweight action. When this happens, rpm goes down to 1,800 or 2,000 rpm, and if you check your engine's power charts you'll see that at full throttle, power is proportional to rpm. With a loss of 500 or 600 rpm, you've got very little power. And with the blades locked in high pitch, raising the nose to climb only slows the rpm down further.

Woodward CSSA governors are spring-loaded to go to the high-rpm position when a cable failure occurs (providing any residual cable friction/tension that might be present can be overcome by the spring), but current regulations do not require governor makers to incorporate such a spring, and many governors now in service do not incorporate this simple fail-soft feature. Even if they did, however, you would not be protected in the event of a serious governor internal breakdown. Lack of oil pressure at the governor's "out" port means a loss of rpm in most aircraft.

Removal and Replacement

All governors mount the same way (since all AND 20010 mounting pads are alike). To dismount a governor, disconnect the control rod or cable at the governor control lever; then remove the four mounting nuts from the hold-down studs and pull the governor straight off the engine. It's as simple as that.

When the governor is off the engine, the drive pad should be covered with plastic or cardboard, or some other suitable makeshift dust cover, to keep soot and dirt out of the engine. The same goes for the governor's drive end. Keep it covered up.

On installation, wipe the engine pad clean. Coat the MS 100009 mounting gasket with Dow Corning DC-7 compound or equivalent and install the gasket onto the engine drive pad. Do not use sealants (RTV) of any kind. After the gasket is in place, install the governor to it, seeing that the splines on the governor shaft engage the drive splines in the engine. (Do not use force.) Finally, install four plain washers and self-locking nuts on the studs and tighten evenly (alternately) to 20 foot-pounds. Attach the control cable to the actuator arm, being sure the full range of travel is available in the cockpit. (Check for binding and/or lost motion; and be sure to leave a 1/8-inch "cushion" at the instrument panel with the knob full-forward.)

More Information

As we say, even A&Ps cannot legally do governor repairs, but if you want to have complete maintenance specifications—including service limits, dimensional data, and torque specifications—for your governor, by all means order the appropriate literature from the factory. The maintenance manual for the CSSA-series Woodward governor is known as Bulletin No. 33001B and is available free from Woodward Governor Co., 5001 N. Second St., Chicago, IL 60615 (312/324-1114)—but enclose $2.00 for postage and handling anyway.

Literature on McCauley governors can be ordered straight from Cessna (or your local Cessna dealer). The complete McCauley Governors and Accumulators Overhaul and Parts Manual is $15. Order P/N 780401-13 from Cessna Aircraft Co., Customer Services Dept., P.O. Box 1521, Wichita, KS 67201.

For information on Hartzell products, write: TRW Hartzell, P.O. Box 1458, Piqua, OH 45356 (phone 513/778-4200).

For information on governor overhaul and exchange (prices vary with make and model), consult Trade-A-Plane or contact Alamo Accessories Inc., 10843 Vandale, San Antonio, TX 78216 (phone 512/349-9721). Alamo is an FAA repair station for accessories and can overhaul or repair any of the popular makes/models of aircraft prop governors. If your governor is not "popular" (e.g., Hamilton Standard), we suggest calling your favorite prop shop or B&S Aircraft Parts and Accessories in Wichita (1414 S. Moseley, KS 67211, phone 1-800-835-2961).

Part III

GETTING THE MOST ENGINE LIFE

Chapter 6

GETTING TO TBO
(AND BEYOND)

Of all the cost-cutting strategies open to plane owners, few are as seductive as TBO-busting—that is, operating one's engine(s) past the manufacurer's recommended "time between overhauls." With engine reserves for even small engines approaching $10 an hour, it's little wonder that every airport ramp now boasts at least one airplane whose Lycoming or Continental is past the magic TBO number.

But how wise is TBO-busting? And how magic is that magic number? Does exceeding the recommended TBO mean having to face a more expensive overhaul later? Is engine reliability seriously degraded by operating on the "back side" of the wear curve? Is there anything one can do to enghance engine longevity, and make TBO-busting a risk-free affair? Judging from our editorial mail, these and similar questions are foremost in the minds of a great many cost-

conscious plane owners. Unfortunately, neat and simple answers are hard to come by, since what's right for one operator, operating one kind of engine, may not be right for another operator with a different kind of engine (or even an engine of the same kind).

Still, there are a few simple truths (and a few subtleties) one should be aware of. TBO-busting will, in fact, net big bucks for some—small bucks for others (and negative bucks for a few). It depends on the kind of engine you have. And how much you know about it.

Two Schools

There are two mains schools of thought on TBO-busting. On the one hand, there are those who would tell you than manufacturers' TBOs are sacrosanct and should never be violated, since they're based on wear rates deduced from millions of hours of real-world experience with tens of thousands of engines. On the other hand, there are those who would say, quite to the contrary, that the manufacturers' TBOs are mainly "paper" numbers—mere guesstimates of engine life—that are influenced by marketing considerations and often have nothing at all to do with the real world (and therefore can and should be ignored).

Our view—one held, we think, by the majority of engine overhaulers—is that the truth lies somewhere in the middle. "All engine models have different relability factors," points out Victor Sloan of Victor Aviation, a premier west-coast engine rebuilder whose customer list includes, among others, Bob Hoover. "Depending on the individual engine and who operates it, the factory TBO may or may not be appropriate. Some TBOs ought to be revised downward, I think. Others maybe ought to be revised upwards. You take an early 'C' model Continental GTSIO-520, for instance—the book TBO and reality are two different things. But some engines are capable of going beyond TBO. It depends on a lot of factors—the type of engine, the operating environment, the quality of the previous overhaul, and so forth."

How are TBOs decided? Only the factory (Lycoming or Contenental) knows for sure—and their decisions are reported in service bulletins (Lycoming S.I. 1009 and Continental M82-9 Rev. 1) which are generally updated once a year. Such factors as engine power output and crankshaft speed, known wear rates (of bearing materials, gears, etc.), and field experience accumulated by fleet operators are all taken into consideration. But in the end, the factory-suggested TBO is, in fact, nothing more than that: a suggestion.

The Cessna 152's O-235-L2C/N2C engine has the longest factory-recommended TBO of any general aviation piston engine, at 2,400 hours. Many other engines can go as long, with proper care.

"These overhaul periods are recommended only," states Continental Service Bulletin M82-9 Rev. 1. "They are not mandatory. They are predicated on compliance with all applicable service bulletins and ADs as well as all required preventive maintenance, periodic inspections, manufacturer's specifications, and the determination by a qualified mechanic that the engine is operating normally and is airworthy."

Under FAR Part 91 rules, TBOs are voluntary—engines do not legally *have* to overhauled, ever. (They must merely be kept airworthy.) Commercial operators are subject to different rules. Part 135 (air taxi) aircraft, in particular, *must* adhere to published TBOs, unless TBO extensions are obtained from the local FAA office.

TBO Extensions

As it turns out, increasing numbers of air taxi operators are going the TBO-extension route (for the same reasons, as non-commercial operators)—with FAA's full blessing. Piper, for example found in a survey of commercial operators of Navajo Chieftain aircraft (which is powered by twin 350-hp Lycoming engines) that actual TBOs among fleet operators are averaging 2,500 hours—some 700 hours more than the TIO-540-J2BD's nominal TBO.

"We do a fair amount of business with commuter airlines," says Victor Aviation's Vic Sloan. "And we've worked with several customers to obtain TBO extensions, generally on the large Continentals, such as the TSIO-520-VB and GTSIO-520-M used on the Cessna 402 and 404. What we do is schedule a fairly detailed phase inspection every 750 hours, and top-overhaul as necessary. We follow oil analysis, and thoroughly borescope each cylinder, and go from there. With good phase checks, some of the GTSIOs have gone 2,000 hours or more between majors. The original versions of those engines were TBO'd at just 1,200 hours."

Another operator who has succeeded in doubling the effective TBO of his Continental engines is William W. Shepherd, a Caterpillar dealer in Los Angeles. Shepherd ran his Cessna 421's engines (375-hp GTSIO-520-Ds) more than 2,300 hours before overhauling them— quite a feat, in view of the fact that the large, geared Continentals are considered by many to be among the most finicky engines in general aviation. Many opertors have trouble achieving the GTSIO-520's old

Ironically, such stalwarts as the Lycoming O-320 (used in the Cessna Skyhawk) may not be good candidates for TBO-busting, if bulletins pertaining to oil pump and valve train have not been complied with. Sintered-iron oil pump gears, for example, must come out at 2,000 hours (under AD 81-18-04). It only makes sense to major the engine when this AD is due.

TBO of 1,200 hours—let alone 2,300-plus. The secret: detailed phase inspections.

Shepherd's first 650-hour check showed that exhaust valves and guides were wearing rapidly (a common problem in large Continentals). These parts were replaced. Then at 1,350 hours, valves and guides were again replaced. Oil analysis and borescope inspections were performed periodically for the next 1,000 hours. When the -H engines were swapped for factory-zero-timed -L engines at 2,300-plus hours, cylinder compression was still good. "Perhaps because there are so many numbers associated with flying," Shepherd speculates, "many piople believe there is some magical quality to TBO. But the TBO on the GTSIO-520 magically was increased by 33.3 percent overnight not long ago; probably because someone decided that, competitively, it was the thing to do."

Maine Aviation Corporation in Portland, Maine (to name one more example) also has met with success in getting the TBOs of Continental engines upped. The firm's engine shop received FAA approval for a 500-hour increase in the TBO of the IO-470 engines on a heavily used Beech Baron, based on a 2,000-hour inspection of two such engines which showed that all cylinders, pistons, cranks, and cams were well within service limits.

The Indestructible O-320s

Probably no engine has done so much to advance the cause of TBO-busting, however, as the O-320 Lycoming. Gifted with cool-running cylinders, sodium-filled exhaust valves, and apparently bullet-proof main bearings, the O-320s seem capable of TBOs much longer than the Lycoming-sanctioned 2,000 hours. On almost any airport, one can find a Cherokee or Cessna 172 owner who has gone 2,200, 2,500, even 3,000 hours between majors.

"I operated an O-320-E2D to 2,700 hours TT without *any* engine work," reports one operator in California. "I sold the airplane, and the new owner put on another 100 hours. The engine, however, was subject to the 1981 oil-pump AD, so the owner did a major overhaul at the time of AD compliance. The engine was within or close to new limits. It was reassembled as *standard* on cylinders and bearings. I had used the airplane for rental and instruction. I have heard of the O-320 being run to 4,000 hours. I believe it could be run to 5,000 hours with one top."

Another reader (the owner of a 1971 Piper Cherokee 140D) confirms the impression of the O-320-E2D. "When I bought my airplane," he says, "it had 1,500 hours on it. The aircraft was used principally in cross-country and instrument flight training; the engine was never top-overhauled. I flew it to 2,138 hours, then had it overhauled by Victor Aviation Services in Palo Alto, California. The reason I had the overhaul done was that I became scared about the oil pump impeller drive shaft. When mine was torn down, the mechanic estimated that I had about five more hours to go...When inquiring around various airports prior to having mine overhauled, I heard many reports of the Lycoming O-320s going well beyond TBO. In fact, one shop at San Jose had recently overhauled an engine that had gone 3,800 hours, claiming there were no problems in the engine."

Even the O-320-H (reviled by many for its history of chewing up camshaft lobes and tappets) seems to be capable of extended-TBO service—with a little luck. "Aside from normal maintenance," reports a billings, Montana Cessna 172N owner, "the only major problem with our plane was a top on cylinders one and three in March 1982. The engine now has 2,600 hours on it and at the last 100-hour, the compression checked 74, 75, 76, 77."

Embry-Riddle Aeronautical University routinely operates O-320 engines (in Cessna 172 training aircraft) to 2,500 hours between majors. Similarly, the University of Illinois has repeatedly run Lycoming O-360-A4M engines (another engine revered for its overall reliability and ruggedness) to 2,500 hours and beyond—with components found well within service limits on teardown.

Nor are small Lycomings the only "flat fours" held in esteem. Small Continentals are held by many to be among the sturdiest of all GA engines. One 1977 Cessna 150 owner claims: "I have personally operated a Continental O-200-A engine to 3,100 hours TT since new. The only work done on the engine was at 598 hours, when three cylinders were replaced under warranty and the remaining cylinder was top-overhauled. From that point on, no cylinders were removed until the engine change at 3,101.5 TTSN."

In general, small displacement and low TTSN equals good TBO potential.

Riley Disagrees

There seems to be a growing consensus among operators and mechanics that an engine with a good service history can safely be pushed beyond TBO if certain parameters are closely followed (e.g., oil analyses, compression, oil consumption), and if periodic checks show no problems. Not everyone agrees with this approach, however. Jack Riley, Jr., president of RAM Aircraft Engine Co. in Waco, Texas (the famous modification center) does not advise his customers to exceed manufacturers' TBOs. According to Riley, an engine's "vital signs" may be within acceptable limits, but because some components are incapable of being monitored by the usual means (borescope, compression testing, etc.), the only way to detect/correct excessive wear is to open up the engine.

"There are a lot of parts in these powerplants that are each doing only a small part of the total work," Riley explains. "If one part malfunctions or fails, the load shifts to others. Eventually, a cumulative-type massive problem or catastrophic failure may occur."

Riley even goes so far as to suggest that general aviation may be demanding too much performance from "seasoned technology" type engines. Turbocharging, high-altitude operation (which gives poor cylinder cooling because of the low air density), added accessories (heavy-duty vacuum pumps, alternators, etc.—all of which require horsepower), and other demands have led to engines in which cylinder heads, valves, pistons, rings, and other components are being subjected to higher stress levels than the engine's designers may originally have had in mind 20 or 30 years ago. For these reasons, Riley is an avowed conservative on TBOs.

Riley is typical of the many overhaulers who feel that current manufacturers' TBOs, far from being too restrictive, are actually in many cases too optimistic—too lenient—considering the limitations of the existing technology. (Donald Bigler, chairman of GAMA and president of Teledyne Continenetal Motors, remarked in a speech to the Aerospace Analysts Society: "Air-cooled engines are at the peak of their development and cannot be rated dependably beyond 2,000 hours.") Which raises an important question: Just what *are* the technological limits to current powerplant TBOs?

Technological Limits

Obviously, there has to be a point beyond which no piston aircraft engine can be operated reliably—a point beyond which *something* is going to wear out, melt, or fatigue-fail. The question is, what *is* that "something"—and at what point (3,000 hours? 5,000 hours?) does it fail? There is no single answer, of course; each engine has its own characteristic weak spot(s), which may differ from those of other engines. A complete discussion of the relevant limiting factors for each and every GA engine family is beyond the scope of this article (although a few of the better-known "limiting factors" for the two or three dozen most popular engines are given later in this chapter).

In general, however, the following rules of thumb seem to hold true:

1. Accessories wear out faster than engines. This is particularly true of magnetos (any brand) and turbochargers.

2. Chromed and nitride-hardened cylinder walls are slower to wear than plain steel bores. But regardless of construction, low-speed, low-compression engines give longer cylinder life than high-speed, high-output engines.

3. Exhaust valves are a major trouble area (from the standpoint of "top end" durability) for air-cooled piston engines. Valve guide wear is also critical.

4. Solid-stemmed exhaust valves such as found in some 0-235 Lycomings—and *all* Continental engines—run 200 to 300 degrees (F) hotter than sodium-filled exhaust valves. As a result, they wear out faster. This is, in our opinion, why Continental engines so often require top overhauls en route to TBO.

5. Sodium-filled exhaust valves are capable of extended service, but the valve-to-guide fit is extremely critical since proper valve cooling depends on dissipation of heat through stem/guide contact. When guide clearance opens up, the valve overheats, wear increases, and (as the worn guide admits hot oil) valve sticking can become a problem.

6. Lead buildup is a key limiting factor in the life of exhaust valves. Accordingly, engines that operate on high-lead 100 or 115/145 avgas can expect short valve life and frequent top-overhauls (unless extra lead scavenger, such as TCP, is added to the fuel). Engines that can use unleaded autogas should see improved exhaust-valve longevity.

7. In Lycoming engines, sintered-iron oil pump impellers and oil pumps with Woodruff-key drives are definite liabilities, where TBO is concerned. No Lycoming engine should be run past TBO unless it has an oil pump of the latest, approved configuration.

8. The more frequent the engine's operation, the better. Lycoming's published TBOs are based on the steady accumulation of *at least* 15 hours of flying time per month. (For some engines, such as the IO-720 and TIO-540-J2BD series, Lycoming allows TBO extensions of 200 hours, providing the engines fly 60 hours per month.) Everyone agrees that inactivity is a detriment to achieving long TBOs.

9. First-run engines (engines that have gone through no previous

Sintered-iron oil pump gears (left) were installed in a wide variety of Lycoming engines from 1975 to 1981. Their service record is poor, and as a result, AD 81-18-04 requires their removal no later than 2,000 hours. Engines that contain sintered-iron impellers are not good candidates for TBO-busting.

overhauls) are conceded to be better risks for TBO-busting than powerplants that have been majored several times before (and that, therefore, contain many high-time parts).

10. With few exceptions, "bottom end" parts outlast "top end" components. Crankshafts, camshafts, tappets, cases, and accessory drives are generally sturdier than most pilots give them credit for. Even such wearing parts as main bearings and rod bearings are usually vastly underrated.

D-I-Y Phase Inspection

The decision whether or not to bust TBO should involve a multiplicity of considerations: Is the engine a first-time runout, or a "senior" several-times-over? (How old is the crank? the cam? the case? The rods?) Have all service bulletins been complied with? (Do you have the latest-style oil pump? Rod bolts? Crankcase? Tappets? Exhaust valves?) Was the previous major overhaul done to service limits, or new limits? Has the engine been run mostly on low-lead fuel, or high-lead? Has oil consumption been trending upward, or staying flat? Has the engine always received regular maintenance? Have filters been changed regularly and often? Is the plane operated conservatively? (No crop dusting or aerobatics; no high-speed letdowns; no chronic overleaning; and no rapid temperature fluctuations.) Is the engine's operating record "clean' with regard to prop stikes, overspeeds, overboost, overtemp, etc.?

Once a decision has been reached to go beyond TBO, it only makes sense to conduct thorough phase checks at preset intervals. You can do such checks yourself, or you can have your repair shop do them. Our own "do-it-yourself" phase-inspection checklist would include the following items:

—Every 25 to 50 hours: oil change; oil filter change (with inspection of contents of old filter); spark plug rotation (and cleaning, if required) with inspection of firing ends for unusual deposits; external visual inspection of engine (for leaks, cracks, etc.) and exhaust, intake, and ignition systems, in accordance with aircraft service manual recommendations. In addition, spectrum analysis should be performed on drain oil.

—Every 100 hours (or earlier): All of the above, plus magneto-to-engine timing check; differential compression check (investigate any cylinder below 50/80); clean and regap spark plugs; replace air filter; borescipe cylinders to check cylinder wall condition (no scoring or step-wear), head condition (no cracks), piston (no burning, cracking), and valves (no erosion or unusual discoloration). Engine should be washed at this time and run up for oil leak inspection. If fuel-injected, all nozzles should come out for cleaning.

—At 1,000 hours SMOH or TTSN, and each 200 hours thereafter: All of the above, plus removal of rocker covers to check for rocker shaft/bushing wear, rocker condition, possible cracks in head castings, evidence of lack of lubrication, overheating, etc; check valve-to-guide clearance i/a/w procedures outlined in Lycoming Service Instruction No. 1088 (replace guides if needed); check pushrod length and/or valve height (solid-tappet engines only); drop exhaust manifold and check exhaust ports for cracking, and look at valves behind face for evidence of necking, erosion, or galling; remove prop and desludge crankshaft oil return hole (constant-speed-prop engines only); check calibration of manifold-pressure, tach, EGT, CHT, and oil-temperature gauges, and correct deficiencies; check for full static rpm; check for unusual noises or vibrations. Magneto internal condition should be checked at this time (points, E-gap, coil condition, etc.) and any deficiencies corrected.

Throughout all above checks, copious notes should be made (preferably, although not necessarily, in the engine logbook) so that on successive inspections, trends can be noted.

Naturally, when anything suspicious is noted (be it a crankcase crack, a downward-trending cylinder, or lack of power in the air), an appropriate investigation should be made, and the decision to continue beyond TBO reevaluated.

Always have in mind a clear plan of action in the event of major trouble—or even in the event of *no* trouble. Determine well in advance exactly how long you intend to continue your experiment. Consider all the factors, then pick your *own* maximum TBO (probably 10 to 50 percent beyond the manufacturer's TBO, depending on the type of engine) . . . and stick with it.

Remember that a high-performance engine that has previously been majored to service limits (rather than new limits), perhaps more than once, is almost alwyas a poor candidate for TBO-busting, particularly if it is more than ten years old, and particularly if the past operating history is not known.

TBO RISK FACTORS: AN ENGINE-BY-ENGINE ASSESSMENT

Each engine family is subject to certain *caveats* where TBO is concerned. The presence or absence of half-inch valves, compliance with ADs, old-style vs. new-style oil pumps, small tappets vs. large tappets, light case vs. heavy case—these and many other factors become a part of the total TBO equation. It is impossible to list all TBO factors, for all engines. Nonetheless, here are some important factors to consider for a few of the most popular engines:

Avco Lycoming

Note: O-235 thru IO-540 Lycoming engines built between 1970 and 1981 may contain sintered-iron oil pump impellers. As a result, such engines may be subject to AD 81-18-04, which requires replacement of iron impellers at 2,000 hours. If you have sintered iron oil pump gears in your engine, no attempt should be made to "bust" TBO. Such gears are a definite hazard and should be removed as soon as practicable.

O-235-C/E/H: Where solid-stem exhaust valves and bronze guides are used, expect to achieve recommended TBO (2,000 hrs.) only with difficulty. Solid-tappet engine requires frequent valve adjustments to make TBO. Plain-steel jugs (not nitrided) give average wear. Chroming not recommended (rings not available). Lead buildup can be severe with high-lead fuels.

O-235-L2C: Nitrided cylinders and sodium valves give good longevity, but solid tappets require careful valve maintenance, and use of high-lead 100 "green" gas may shorten top-end life. (TCP will help, though.) Chroming of cylinders not recommended, due to unavailablility of suitable rings.

O-320-A/C/E: Engines built before 1967 may have 7/16" exhaust valves, in which case the recommended TBO of 1,200 hours should be adhered to. Because these engines do not tolerate lead well, Lycoming advises restricting use of "green" 100-octane gas to 25 percent of total operating time or less. With TCP and use of 1/2" valves, a 2,000-hour TBO can be met or exceeded (except aerobic engines). Nitrided cylinders not available for -A models.

O-320-B/D: High-compression versions of -A/C/E models which tolerate lead better. However, high-time cylinder heads are apt to develop small cracks. The jugs may either be chromed or nitrided and thus wear good. First-run cylinders can easily exceeded the recommended 2,000 hours.

O-320-H: Unless the large-tappet, large-cam 'T' mods have been done (indicated by a suffix 'T' on the serial number), tappet spalling may be encountered en route to TBO, even if Lycoming oil additive LW-16702 is used. Because of this risk, it is advisable to adhere to factory TBO (2,000 hours)—and convert to 'T' configuration as soon as possible.

IO-320-C1A: These engines have $358 Inconel exhaust valves (to accommodate turbocharging). With proper care, the 1,800-hr TBO can be exceeded. (Nitrided jugs give good service life.)

O-360-E: Early versions of these engines incorporated same tappets and camshafts as O-320-H (see above). Same caution applies.

O-360-A/B/C/D: These are arguably Lycoming's finest engines (for long, reliable service). With nitrided cylinders, and assuming all bulletins/ADs are up to date, expect 2,600 hours TBO; 3,000 for first-run engines.

TO-360-C/F: Cooling problems caused by a relatively poor match of turbocharger to engine gives these Lycomings a factory TBO of 1,400 hours—which is probably a good idea not to exceed.

IO-360-B/E/F: Members of the 180-hp IO-360 group have chrome-stemmed sodium exhaust valves and nitrided cylinders, and a generally stone-solid bottom end. These engines very often exceed the recommended TBO of 2,000 hours.

IO-360-A/C/D/J: The 200-hp IO-360 family uses plain (not chrome-stem) sodium valves. A variety of crankcases can be found. Cases with small main-bearing dowels should not be run past 1,200 hours. Engines with large dowels and old-style camshaft should not exceed 1,400 hours. Late-style engines (with latest cam) can go 1,800 hours or more, but watch for crankcase cracks.

TIO-360-A: Different turbo, controller, and fuel metering system from TO-360 series, but still not a good combo for long engine life. Factory TBO of 1,200 hours should be respected.

AIO-360: Aerobatic engines in this group can go a maximum of 1,200 hours between overhauls (or 1,400 if derated to 180-hp). However, a less optimistic figure probably ought to be chosen if more than occasional aerobatics are performed.

GO-435: Many owners claim they make it beyond the 1,200 TBO. This engine is particularly sensitive to operator technique.

GO-480: Engines modified i/a/w applicable bulletins (e.g.: S.I. 1182A on high-lift rockers and late-style cam) and incorporating sodium-filled valves can exceed the 1,400-hr TBO.

O-540: Older engines may still have 7/16" exhaust valves (and 1,200-hr TBO). Chromed sodium 1/2" valves are used in the majority, however, and TBOs in excess of the recommended 2,000 hours are not uncommon. Frequent oil changes and careful attention to valve and guide clearance (see Service Instruction No. 1088) are essential to prevent valve sticking, particularly if green gas is used.

IO-540-E1A5: The updraft-cooling, top-exhaust IO-540 carries a nominal TBO of 1,400 hours. Frankly, we can't understand why. The engine—in our opinion—deserves a much higher TBO (unless Rajay turbos are used; then subtract 200 hours).

IO-540: TBO can often be exceeded if all bulletins/ADs are complied with and the engine is given careful maintenance, particularly if low-lead fuel is used.

TIO-540-A/C: Engines made before 1971 (or not modified to large main bearing dowels i/a/w S.I. 1225) should not be operated past 1,500 hours. Late-style engines often exceed the recommended 1,800-hr TBO (many go as long as 2,400 hours), although periodic turbo repairs may be needed.

TIO-540-J/F/N/R: The 350-hp versions develop more heat than other TIO-540s; hence, recommended TBO is only 1,600 hours (1,800 if operated in air-taxi service). With careful maintenance, 2,400 hours can be achieved. Watch for crankcase cracks, however.

TIO-541-E: Engines shipped after March 1976, and those updated to the latest case and cylinder configurations i/a/w S.B. 334 and 353, are eligible for a 1,600-hr TBO. (This has been exceeded by some opeators.) Early-style engines should go no more than 1,200 hours.

TIGO-541: Factory TBO of 1,200 hours is pure fiction. Cooling problems, spur gear, high rpms spell trouble. Try 800 hours.

IO-720: Cylinders are straight from IO-360-A1A, bottom end is sturdy, and—consequently—TBOs beyond 2,000 hours are eminently possible.

Teledyne Continental

O-200-A: Recommended TBO is 1,800 hours. With close adherence to bulletins and use of low-lead or unleaded fuels, TBOs much higher should be routine. Basically a viceless engine whose potential is limited only by exhaust-valve (and guide) life.

O-300: Average engine makes TBO (1,800 hrs.), but many are now old and tired and can look forward to cracking problems, with both heads and cases. Valve sticking can occur with high-lead fuels, particularly as bronze guides wear out.

GO-300: Geared version of O-300. Higher rpms lead to hotter operation (definitely a drawbacks). Spur gear at front of case needs attention after 1,200 hours. Crankcase cracks are possible. TBO-busting not recommended.

E-185/225: Basically early O-470s with parallel-valve heads and three-ring pistons. These engines do poorly on high-lead fuels, but can make the recommended 1,500 hours if 80-octane or unleaded autogas is used. Not a good candidate for TBO-busting. Frequent exhaust valve problems.

IO-360: Engines made before 1976 should not be run past the recommended TBO of 1,500, unless updated to latest configuration. (An improved crankcase became available in 1976. Heavier crankshaft started in 1979. Numerous other changes have been made as well.)

IO-360-KB: Continental says 2,000 hours. (The 'B' models have the heavy crank.) We agree.

TSIO-360-A/B/C: Factory TBO of 1,400 hours should probably be raised to 1,600 or 1,800 (at least for fully updated models, with '-B' crank and late case). Watch exhaust valves for necking, burning.

TSIO-360-E/F/G: These engines are hot-running (due to fixed-wastegated Rajay turbo) and hard on pistons. Watch for valve burning, rocker bushing wear, and tach drive breakage. Significant service bulletins affect turbo, mags, oil pump, and crankshaft. Not a good candidate for TBO-busting. (Factory says 1,800 hours. That should probably be revised downward.)

O-470: Exceptionally strong "bottom end." Low compression ratios (and power output) translate to long engine life. Good candidates for TBO-busting if low-lead fuels (and TCP) are used. Many operators exceed 1,500-hr TBO. Watch for exhaust valve necking, burning, guide wear.

IO-470: With "heavy" cylinders, another good candidate for exceeding the factory's 1,500-hr TBO. Again, exhaust valves must be watched closely.

TSIO-470: Official TBO of 1,400 hours is optimistic for cylinders, pessimistic for bottom end. Turbocharging creates added heat burden for valves.

IO-520: Limiting factors in achieving 1,700-hr recommended TBO are exhaust valve (and guide) wear, and case cracking. So-called "heavy" cases still crack. Permold cases (alternator at right front cylinder) are somewhat more crack-prone than sandcast cases (which have oil cooler up front). Crank and main bearings are probably good for 3,000 to 4,000 hours.

TSIO-520-NB: One of the best "big Continentals," intercooled and matched to a good turbo. Continental says 1,600 hours; with pressurized mags and top-end work as needed (to correct and/or prevent valve problems), we say 2,000 to 2,400 hours.

TSIO-520-UB/VB/WB/AF: Continental allows 1,600 hours' TBO for these models—vs. 1,400 for other TSIO-520s—apparently on the strength of recent top-end mods, but only the -WB has intercooling, and it alone seems to us a good bet for TBO-busting. (Even so, exhaust valves bear watching.) The non-intercooled models run hot and hard. A 1,600-hr TBO seems optimistic.

TSIO-520-AE: The lightweight Cessna Crusader engine is rated for 2,000 hours, based on top-end improvements and low power output. Time will tell, of course, but we remain a trifle skeptical of the factory-specified TBO.

TSIO-520-R: The Cessna P210 engine, though gifted with a strong bottom end, is notorious for not making TBO (1,400 hours). Don't push your luck.

TSIO-520: Standard TSIO-520s without intercooling and not incorporating nitralloy guides, high-flow exhaust valve lifters, etc., are not good candidates for TBO-busting, particularly if the bottom end incorporates old-style, small main bearings and crank (i.e, no 'B' suffix to the model designator), and particularly if the crankcase is an early-generation Permold. Standard steel jugs tend to lose their choke fast; the 1,400-hour factory TBO should probably be respected.

GTSIO-520-L/M/N: Factory now says 1,600 hours (based on recent improvements to pistons, valves, guides, lifters, case, and piston pins). With adequate attention to exhaust valves, we agree; in fact, the bottom end is probably capable of 2,400 hours or more. Operator technique will definitely make a difference.

GTSIO-520-F/K: The Aero Commander 685 engines are among Continental's most expensive, and shortest-lived. We know of no one who has made the 1,200-hr TBO. The thought of trying to bust TBO with these engines borders on abject lunacy.

GTSIO-520: For all other GTSIO-520s (including early -L models without the latest updates), Continental says 1,200 hours is the best TBO. But if you've made it to 1,200 and all indicators are "go," by all means shoot for 1,600. The bottom end is strong; chief obstacle to higher TBOs is heat damage to valves, pistons, rings. On second-run and older engines, keep a sharp lookout for cracks (everywhere) as you approach TBO. Operator technique is extremely important. Fly conservatively, and invest in meticulous accessory maintenance (mags, turbos, etc.).

PRE-ASSEMBLY LUBRICATION

We have no hard numbers to draw on regarding the number of engines that experience component failure(s) immediately following (i.e., within 100 hours of) top or major overhaul; but if the stern warning given on page 3-3 of Lycoming's direct-drive engine *Overhaul Manual* is any indication, the numbers must be alarming. Says Lycoming: "Many premature failure of parts have been traced directly to improper prelubrication at engine assembly. If parts are not properly lubricated, or an inferior lubricant is used, many of the engine parts will become scored before the engine oil goes through its first cycle and has had a chance to lubricate the engine. This, of course, will

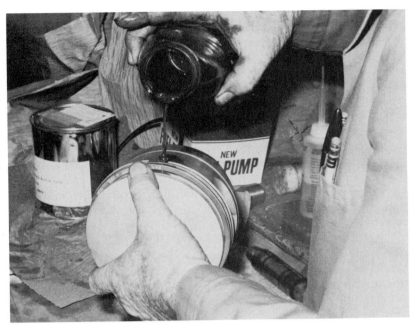

During engine buildup, parts should be coated with heavy-weight engine oil (SAE 50 or higher). STP blends, still popular in many shops, are probably best avoided.

lead to premature parts failure...and in some cases, engine failure before normal service hours have been accumulated."

The question thus arises: What constitutes proper prelubrication during overhaul? Which parts should be lubed? And with what?

As usual, everyone you ask has a different answer to each of these question. The FAA, in AC 65-12A, says merely to coat engine parts "with oil." Lycoming, on the other hand, specifically states in one of its manuals: "The practice of using plain lubricating oil during assembly is not recommended." Lycoming and Continental have their own ideas about how to prelubricate parts, and quite often their recommendations differ. Then too, many mechanics have developed their own preferred prelube tricks, which often bear no relationship to anything described in the manufacturers' overhaul manuals.

One thing is certain: Everyone agrees on the need for prelubrication of moving (and "rubbed against") parts prior to assembly. Any attempt to run an engine without prelubing of piston pins, cylinder walls, valves, guides, tappet faces, etc., will almost certainly end in disaster . . . eventually.

Continental's primary prelube recommendation (made in the "Final Assembly" section of most of its shop manulas) is: "Apply clean engine lubrication oil liberally to all bare steel surfaces, journals, bearings, and bushings before and/or after installation . . . except where special lubricants are recommended." Some instances in which special prelubricants are, indeed, recommended include valve stems in guides (which are to be greased with Shell Alvania No. 2), rocker arm feet (to be lubed with Molyshield Grease by American Lubricating Co., P.O. Box 696, Dayton, OH 45401), and cylinder walls of plain-steel jugs (which should be coated "thoroughly with Lubriplate No. 2, Sunoco way oil, or castor oil"). For *chromed* cylinders, Contienental recommends a rub-down with SAE 50-weight non-detergent mineral oil. According to Contenental Service Bulletin M73-24, "The use of heavy viscosity [lubricants] and additives is not recommended unless cylinders will not be run for an extended period." By additives, Continental presumably means STP.

Lycoming recommends that machined-steel surfaces be lubricated with *preservative* oil (not engine oil) prior to assembly, since machined steel is particularly quick to corrode (i.e., rust) upon exposure to atmospheric moisture (to say nothing of the moisture and salts in skin perspiration). Preservative oil conforming to MIL-C-6529 can be obtained through any oil jobber. Some familiar names are Exxon Rust-Ban and Cosmoline 1223.

Nitrided-steel and chromed cylinder walls, according to Lycoming, can be coated with a mixture containing 15% prelubricant ("STP or equivalent" in the words of one Lycoming manual) and 855 SAE 50 aviation-grade mineral oil.

High-friction parts such as cam lobes, tappet faces, piston pin plugs, and valve guides (to name but a few) should, according to Lycoming, get a thorough coating of one of the following heavy-duty lubricants:
1. Kendor 155 Compound (by Kendall)
2. Modoc 165 (Atlantic Richfield)
3. Lubri-bond A (Electro Film Incs.)
4. Moly-Tex Grease O (Texaco)
5. Tuban 140 (Texaco)

Lycoming is quick to add that these five lubricants are not necessarily the *only* products than can be used; rather these are just a few of the products that Lycoming factory personnel have "tested and used successfully." (For more information, see Lycoming Service Instruction No. 1059A.)

As mentioned earlier, many mechanics have developed their own favorite "prelubes" for use on cylinder walls, pistons, and rings. Some of the more popular products used in this context are cator oil, STP, and automotive transmission fluid, used undiluted or combined in various proportions with non-detergent engine oil. Generally speaking, most mechanics match the viscosity of the prelube to the expected length of tie the engine will remain inoperative (i.e., the longer the anticipated wait for return-to-service, the thicker the prelube). Straight 40 or 50-weight mineral oil is often used when the engine is to be put back in operation within a day or two. When it is known that the engine will remain grounded for several days (or weeks), a mix of STP (or an equivalent product) and 50-weight av oil is often used. In addition, special pre-oiling techniques (such as those called out in Lycoming Service Instruction No. 1241) are frequently employed to prevent damage in overhauled engines that have been allowed to sit for some time prior to startup.

It should also be mentioned that many of the big cylinder overhaul shops have developed their own secret-formula "make-up oils" and "assembly oils," which may be obtained commercially for use in do-it-yourself top overhauls.

PROTECTION DURING INACTIVITY

"Reports of cylinder wall corrosion," Teledyne Continental Motors warns in a service bulletin, "appear to be increasing. It is a proven fact that engines in aircraft that are flown only occasionally tend to exhibit this problem much more than engines in aircraft that are flown frequently.

"Of particluar concern are new engines or engines with new or freshly honed cylinders after a top or major overhaul. In areas of high humidity, there have been instances where corrosion has been found in such cylinders after an inactive period of *only a few days*. Once these cylinders have been operated for approximately 50 hours, the varnish which collects on the cylinder walls offers some protection against this possibility.

"Obviously," the Continental bulletin continues, "proper steps must be taken on engines used infrequently to preclude the possiblity of corrosion. This is especially true if the aircraft is based near the sea

Lycoming allows a 200-hr increase in recommended TBO for operators of certain engines (such as the Navajo's TIO-540-J2BD) when utilization is at least 60 hours a month. Inactivity, not activity, results in a low TBO.

coast or in areas of high humidity and not flown more than once a week."

Both of the Big Two general aviation engine manufacturers agree that the best, most effective method of preventing engine internal corrosion is to fly the aircraft often—the oftener, the better. As fuel-production shortfalls grow worse, however—and as sterner conservation measures begin to take hold—fewer and fewer pilots will be flying their engines as often as they should (or want to) in the weeks and months ahead. Which means that corrosion is going to exact an ever-heavier toll on aircraft engines, *unless* pilots take appropriate steps to preserve their engines during periods of inactivity—including *short* periods of inactivity.

The first thing you can do to protect your engine (and this is something you should already be doing) is rotate the prop by hand serveral revolutions every week or so, to dispell any beads of moisture that might have formed on the cylinder walls and redistribute oil on the walls. Continental recommends turning the prop a total of five revolutions every seven days; Lycoming recommends the same procedure every *five* days. According to Lycoming Service Letter L180, "ground running the engine for brief periods of time is not a substitute for turning the engine over by hand; in fact, the practice of ground running will tend to aggravate rather than minimize corrosion formation in the engine."

Obviously, you'll want to have the keys in your pocket (and the plane chained to the ground) when you go about turning the propeller by hand. Also, as a safety precaution, you should rotate the prop *backwards,* so that the impulse couplings in your mags (assuming you have impulse couplings, rather than retard points) won't trip. Remember that if either of your magnetos has a broken P-lead, the engine is "hot" and may well fire up as you move the prop. Take appropriate precautions.

Continental offers specific suggestions for preserving the engine of an aircraft that will be inactive for from 7 to 30 days; these suggestions pertain to what is called "flyable storage." (Separate recommendations are given for "temporary storage," which is for inactive periods of up to—but not more than—90 days. In addition, there is a procedure to follow for "indefinite storage," involving idle periods of *more than* 90 days.) Continental's "flyable storage" engine-preservation procedure is as follows:

1. Operate the engine (preferably in flight) until the oil tememprature rises to the normal operating range, then—while the engine is still warm—completely drain the oil from the sump and replace the drain plug.

2. Next, fill the sump to the "full" mark on the dipstick using a lubricating oil that meets the requirements of MIL-C-6529, Type II. [*The Type II oil called for can be formulated by mixing one part of MIL-C-6529, Type I (Exxon Rust-Ban 628, Cosmoline 1223, or the equivalent) with three parts of new lubricating oil of the appropriate SAE grade. This mixture, when made using uncompounded oil, is the same oil as Continental recommends be used in all of its new and overhauled engines for the first 25 hours of operation.—Ed.]*

3. Run the engine at least five minutes at an rpm between 1200 and 1500 with the oil tememprature and cylinder head temperature in the normal operating range. (Lycoming engines: Operate until oil temperature reaches at least 180°F, but do not exceed a CHT of 475°F.)

During the flyable-storage period, Continental states that "the propeller shall be rotated by hand [once every seven days] without running the engine." Furthermore, "after rotating the engine six revolutions, stop the propeller 45° to 90° from the position it was in."

Continental recommends that if by the end of 30 days the aircraft has not been taken out of lyable storage (which is accomplished simply by draining the preservative oil and replacing it with the regular grade of engine oil), the engine should be started and run to bring the oil and cylinder temperatures into the green. Preferably, the aircraft should be flown for at least 30 minutes.

When an aircraft is to be left idle for more than 30 days, but less than 90 days, *temporary storage* procedures should be followed. Lycoming's temporary storage recommendations call for the replacement of crankcase oil with MIL-C-6529 (Type I) preservative oil, operation of the engine to bring oil and cylinder temperatures into the green, *draining* the preservative oil from the crankcase (save the oil; you can reuse it), spraying hot preservative oil (MIL-C-6529 Type I at 200°F) into the cylinders while the engine is cranked with the starter (all spark plugs removed), and replacement of the spark plugs with dehydrator plugs.

When the Lycoming "temporary storage" procedure is used, it is essential to place signs and/or red flags in the cockpit and on the propeller stating: "Do not operate engine—no oil in engine" (or something similar to that effect). The crankcase will be empty until oil of the appropriate grade is added to it.

Also, according to Lycoming Service Letter L180, once the plane is ready to be taken out of storage, "it is not necessary to flush preservative oil from the cylinder prior to flying the aircraft. The small quantity of oil coating the cylinders will be expelled from the engine during the first few minutes of operation."

Teledyne Continental's temporary-storage procedure involves the following steps:

1. After removing the top spark plugs, spray MIL-L-46002 (Grade 1) preservative oil, at room temperature, into each cylinder with the piston in the *bottom-dead-center* position. Rotate the crankshaft as necessary when going from one cylinder to the next—but at the end, leave no piston at the top position.

2. Respray each cylinder without moving the crankshaft.

3. Reinstall the spark plugs.

4. Spray approximately two ounces of preservative oil through the oil filler opening in order to coat the engine interior. (Note: The crankcase should contain MIL-C-6529, Type II preservative oil).

5. Placard the propeller with the following notice: "DO NOT TURN PROPELLER. ENGINE PRESERVED."

Regardless of whether the Lycoming or the Continental method is used, it is a good idea—whenever an aircraft is left to sit idle for weeks at a time—to seal all engine cowl openings with close-fitting plugs and attach red streamers at each point. This is particularly true for the exhaust pipes, which will (unless blocked off) admit moisture into the exhaust manifolds and (through open exhaust valves) directly into at least half the engine's cylinders. (Block exhaust tubes with bags of desiccant, and change the bags every few weeks. Don't forget to remove the bags prior to returning the aircraft to service.)

Also, regardless of which method you use, don't forget to cap off the crankcase breather tube (not only at the end, but at any condensation holes along its length). And don't forget to *uncap* it later, before you go flying.

For more information on the subject of engine preservation, consult Avco Lycoming Service Letter L180 and/or TCM Service Bulletin M74-9 (available free from Avco Lycoming, Williamsport, PA 17701 and Teledyne Continental Motors, Box 90, Mobile, AL 36601, respectively).

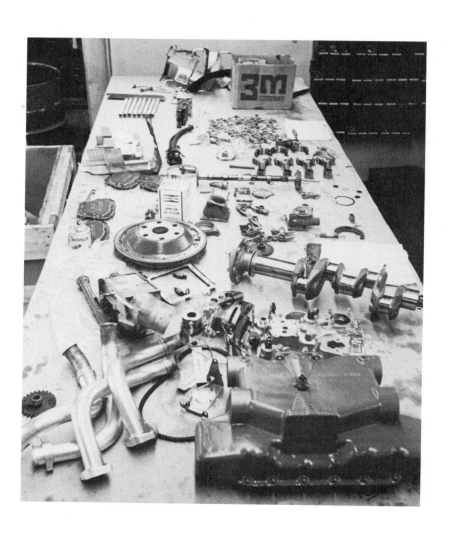

Chapter 7

MAJOR OVERHAUL

It's probably fair to say that few events in the life of a plane-owner are more harrowing (emotionally as well as financially) than removal of the engine for major overhaul. Engine rebuilding is not only frightfully expensive (even the smallest Lycomings can cost $5,000 or more to overhaul properly) but conjures worries about reliability, too. A shoddy overhaul, or one that fails to incorporate the latest service-bulletin mods and ADs, can lead to high oil consumption, an unscheduled top overhaul, or even outright engine failure. The stakes are high indeed.

An exhaustive discussion of the major overhaul is beyond the scope of this book; however, the topic is sufficiently important that it warrants at least some discussion here, particularly with regard to how an owner can best plan (and shop) for a major overhaul. The difference between getting a good overhaul and a poor one is often the difference between shopping knowledgeably, on the one hand, and going with the lowest bidder, on the other.

IMPORTANT TERMS

It's important to understanding exactly what is meant by "major overhaul." The terms "major overhaul," "rebuilt," and "remanufactured" are bandied about rather carelessly by mechanics and overhaulers, but in fact each term has a rather specific meaning.

Major overhaul is an event comprising complete disassembly of the engine, inspection of load-bearing parts, and replacement of wear items, in accordance with the procedures given in the manufacturer's overhaul manual (and any relevant service bulletins). This means, for example, not only dimensional inspection but Magnaflux inspection of the crankshaft (and/or ultrasound inspection, if the engine is a Continental), Zyglo inspection of major reusable aluminum parts (such as the crankcase), and visual inspection of other parts using NDT (non-destructive-test) methods as specified in the factory overhaul manual. In the end, all parts must meet the tolerances spelled out in the manufacturer's Table of Limits, which is generally given in the back of the overhaul manual (but may also be issued as a separate publication).

Regardless of their dimensional characteristics, some parts *must* be trash-canned during major overhaul no matter how much life may be left in them. For example, Lycoming (in Service Bulletin No. 240), lists the following as 100-percent replacement items for all engines at major overhaul:

1. Oil hoses.
2. Oil seals.
3. Gaskets.
4. Cylinder base seals.
5. Circlips, lockplates, and retaining rings.
6. Piston rings.
7. Piston pins (except heavy-wall construction).
8. Piston pin plugs.
9. Prop governor oil line elbows (aluminum only; steel elbows need not be replaced).
10. Prop shaft sleeve rings.
11. Pinion shaft rollers (reduction gear pinion cage, geared engines).
12. Propeller shaft thrust bearings (geared engines).
13. Supercharger bearing oil seal (supercharged engines only).
14. Exhaust valves (all).
15. Exhaust valve retaining keys.
16. Bearing inserts (main and rod).
17. Cylinder fin stabilizers.
18. Magneto drive cushions.
19. Stressed bolts and fasteners (including camshaft gear attach hardware, con rod bolts and nuts, crank flange bolts, and stationary drive gear bolts on reduction gears).
20. Damaged ignition cables.
21. Crankshaft sludge tubes.
22. Counterweight bushings in crankshaft.
23. All fuel-line hoses for IGSO-540-A series engines.
24. Accessory drive coupling springs (supercharged and VO-540 series engines).
25. AC diaphragm-type fuel pumps.

(Note: Lycoming LW-12596 connecting rod bolts may be reused providing they are inspected for galling, and magnetic-particle inspected, and measured to determine that their free length does not exceed 2.249/2.250 inches.)

   Teledyne Continental Motors publishes a comparable listing of mandatory-replacement items in its Service Bulletin M87-11 (currently in its second revision, at press time). Interestingly, Continental mandates the total replacement of hydraulic lifters (or tappets) on all 360-cubic-inch-and-larger engines at overhaul time; Lycoming does not. (Continental also now requires total replacement of pistons. Lycoming does not.)

   Technically speaking, althogh exhaust valves are on the above list, neither Lycoming nor Continental *requires* replacement of valve *guides* at major overhaul, instead requiring only that they meet the tolerances spelled out in the Table of Limits. Even so, any good overhauler will

Only the manufacturer can throw away logbooks and deem a rebuilt engine to be "zero-time." (Photo courtesy Teledyne Continental Motors)

tell you that valve guides seldom meet those tolerances after a 1,500- or 2,000-hour TBO run. Most good shops routinely replace guides as a matter of course, without even inspecting old ones to see if they're still good.

What about the terms "remanufactured" and "rebuilt"? A few years ago, FAA redefined these terms to allow overhaulers in the field to use the word "remanufactured" essentially any way they want. (Before, only the manufacturers could use this term, and it specifically referred to engines that had been granted "zero time" in the course of a factory overhaul.) The term "rebuilt" is now specifically used in reference to engines that have been overhauled to *new limits.*

Conversion of an engine to the latest crankcase configuration can drive overhaul costs up. This Continental IO-520 has a light case, which is subject to an A.D.

(The manufacturers' Tables of Limits contain two categories of tolerances for such things as ring fits, barrel choke, cylinder out-of-round, etc. "New limits" are the tolerances that apply to new engines during original manufacture. "Service limits" are the tolerances that are acceptable for continued use of engine parts in the field.)

Anybody who overhauls an engine can choose to overhaul it to new limits, but only the factory can qualify a rebuilt engine as *zero-timed.* The factory is legally entitled, when it overhauls an engine to new limits, to dispose of the old logbooks and declare the engine to have "zero time" even though it may still contain some previously used components. It's important to understand that, legally speaking, no one but the factory can "zero-time" an engine. When an engine is overhauled by somebody other than the factory, the *old logbooks must be kept in service.* Only the factory can issue new logbooks for an engine.

Obviously, it's of prime importance, when shopping for an overhaul, to determine whether the engine is to be overhauled to new limits or to service limits. The latter is generally cheaper (initially), because more parts can be reused. This often makes good sense; it's not always economically feasible to replace, say, a crankshaft that meets service limits but not "new limits." (A new crankshaft for a Lycoming IO-720 lists for over $20,000. Cranks for many popular engines list for $5,000 to $7,000.) Likewise, in some instances, insisting on a new-limits overhaul will mean scrapping one or more cylinders, if serious barrel wear is evident. In such cases it is almost always more cost-effective to salvage the cylinders by chroming, or grinding oversize. (However, even in the case of a "chrome major," it is possible—and highly advisable—to adhere to new-limits specifications for piston ring sideplay, ring gaps, choke, piston skirt clearance, out-of-round, and other important "top end" tolerances.)

As said earlier, a complete discussion of all the factors relevant to major-overhauling would require more pages than are available here. Meanwhile, we present below some questions that can be used as an aid in shopping for a major overhaul.

20 QUESTIONS FOR YOUR OVERHAULER

The best deal on an overhaul isn't necessarily the cheapest deal—nearly everybody agrees on that—but slogging through the murky waters of overhaulers' hype isn't a simple matter. It's easy to get sidetracked by discussions of warranties, accessory provisions, core charges, shipping, Lord mounts, test-cell run-in, etc.—to say nothing of installation labor and turnaround time.

In the interest of keeping owners out of trouble (and honest overhaulers in business), we've put together a checklist of sorts to aid operators in getting the best possible overhaul for the least possible money. We recommend you try the following questions out on your overhauler (put them in writing and send them off in letter form to any overhaulers you're seriously considering doing business with) and see what you get for a response, before committing to any one facility:

1. What kind of engine do you specialize in? (Or: How many engines of my make and model did you overhaul last year?) Generally speaking, you don't want to take your P-Navajo's Lycoming TIGO-541-E1As to a shop that's never seen anything bigger than an O-200. Find out what the shop's specialty is (Lycoming fours; geared Continentals; round engines; or whatever) and be sure they've done your type of engine before. If they claim that they specialize in "all types of engines," be wary.

2. Do you overhaul to new limits, or service limits? Most shops now claim to overhaul to new limits, but you can cut through the B.S. by asking for a few simple dimensions. The proper "new limits" bore for a 320-, 360-, or 540-series Lycoming cylinder, for example, is 5.125 inches plus .002, minus .005. (The Lycoming "Service Table of Limits" limit of 5.1305-in. is a service limit.) Ask about ring gaps and side clearances, and whether pistons are customarily thrown away and replaced with new. If the shop is in the habit of reusing pistons, as yourself—and them—how they obtain new-limit ring fits with worn piston lands.

3. Do you reuse exhaust valves? The answer here should be a firm no. (Lycoming no longer allows the recycling of Inconel valves.)

4. How much choke do you put in reground cylinders? This is particularly important for O-470 and IO-520 Continental owners. Look for an answer in the .005 to .008-in. range. Anything less than that is an invitation to a top overhaul 500 hours post-major.

5. What style piston-pin plug do you use (Lycoming)? There are three different types of Lycoming wrist-pin plugs in service: the P/N 60828 aluminum plug, P/N 72198 aluminum-bronze, and the LW-

Cylinder bores will be checked for out-of-round, step wear, diameter, and choke (and measurements recorded) prior to rework. In many cases, the diameter after regrinding to restore choke or roundness will put the cylinder out of service limits, making chrome-plating necessary.

11775 "doweled" plug (see Q&A, January '85 for a complete discussion). The plugs are interchangeable and are used in a wide variety of Lycoming models, but the various P/N plugs have widely differing failure rates. You want the doweled plug, in conjunction with heavy-walled P/N 14077 or -14078 wrist pins.

6. What style valve guide do you use? This is a rather lengthy discussion unto itself, but the essence of it is, Lycoming and Continental have each made major changes in exhaust valve and guide materials over the last few years, and generally speaking, you now want your high-output Lycoming or Continental to have Nimonic valves in cast-iron (Ni-resist) guides. (Continental's latest exhaust valve for -470 and -520 engines is P/N 646286.) Nitralloy guides have proven somewhat unpredictable for Continental owners; ask your shop what their experience has been (bear in mind that you have to replace your exhaust lifters with special high-oil-flow variants), and if you decide to go the nitralloy-guide route, be sure you're getting the latest part number (P/N 648014 is current).

7. Do you substitute PMA parts for genuine factory parts? What's my price savings with parts by Superior, Precision, or ECI? This is a sore point, admittedly, because most overhaul shops do use PMA (Parts Manufacturer Approval) parts—aftermarket valves, guides, pistons, rings, etc. (which are often half the cost of Lycoming or Continental equivalents)—and most shops do not want owners knowing about it, because the cost saving, by and large, isn't passed on to the customer. (Ask for a basic price quote on your engine. Then ask for a breakdown into two price quotes based on the use of genuine factory parts or PMA parts.) FAA-PMA parts are generally just as good as—and in some cases slightly better than—factory original parts. But you're the customer, and you should know what you're getting (or not getting), so you can meaningfully compare price quotes from other overhaulers.

8. Do cylinders and valve guides come with proper micro-inch honed finish? (Honing is discussed in detail further below.) Ask for actual micro-inch RMS numbers (answers should be in the 25-40 micro-inch range), and ask if valve guides are honed (to 30 micro-inches RMS) per Lycoming Service Instruction No. 1200A.

9. Who does your crank regrinding? Does it cost extra? Does it include dynamic balancing? Most shops send cranks out for grinding; you want to know that the regrinder has been around awhile, specializes in crank grinding, and is an FAA-certified Repair Station. (AEA

in Dallas and ECI in San Antonio are two of the better-known names in this field.) If your overhauler tells you that the customer must guarantee the crank to be serviceable, what does that mean, exactly? Does that mean it must be regrindable, but the customer pays for any needed regrinding? Does it mean the overhauler pays for regrinding? What about nitriding? Counterweight reconditioning? Magnafluxing? Ultrasound? What if (horror of horrors) your crank is unrepairable? Get it all in writing ahead of time.

10. Will my camshaft be reground? (Lifters?) By whom? Who pays if the cam is found to be worn beyond repair? Who pays if reconditioned lifters start tearing up a cam lobe in 100 hours? Again, get it in writing.

11. What accessories are included in the overhaul price? Who certifies them? Generally, the overhaul price includes the cost of reconditioned-exchange starter, magnetos, harness, carburetor or injector, fuel pumps, and alternator. (Vacuum pumps may or may not be included as well.) Find out for sure whether your carb or injector is to be overhauled, or merely bench-calibrated and yellow-tagged. (Lowball overhaulers generally do not include the cost of a complete Bendix fuel-injector overhaul in their prices.) Who warrantees the accessories?

12. Can I have fine-wire spark plugs at no extra cost? Use this as a bargaining chip as shop-selection time draws near.

13. Who does your cylinder chroming? Can I opt for an oversize grind instead? Chroming isn't something that should be entrusted to just anyone. You want a major shop (such as Schneck or ECI) to do any chrome-plating; otherwise you should opt for an oversize grind, if possible. (Unfortunately, this is not an option for some Lycoming owners; Avco does not allow regrinding of most nitrided jugs.)

14. Will I get to keep my cylinders, or is there a chance they'll be exchanged for somebody else's? To each his own. We prefer to hold onto (and repair) our own cylinders, if possible; we don't want anybody else's recycled junk. (You don't know where it's been.)

15. Will I get a written logbook record indicating compliance with applicable service bulletins by number? The answer better be "yes."

16. Who pays if a cylinder cracks after 100 hours? Answer: They do.

17. Who pays if the crankcase starts leaking oil at a parting line or through-stud? Effective repairs can get hairy; you want some assurance that a leaker will be fixed at no cost to you.

18. How do you run-in your engines, what break-in oil do you use,

Crankshafts often have to be reground to restore roundness to bearing journals. It's important to establish who will bear the cost of regrinding (if it should become necessary), and who will guarantee the crank against defects.

and what are your limits for oil consumption? The answers should be: On a fully instrumented test stand per the manufacturer's published run-in procedure; Shell red-can 50-weight or equivalent; and one quart in three hours, tops.

19. What happens if my engine is still using a quart of oil every two or three hours after a 50-hour break-in period? The answer you're looking for is: "We'll do whatever is necessary to correct an oil-consumption problem." That means deglazing defective cylinders free of charge, replacing any that have cracks, and replacing the replacements if they don't break in in 50 hours.

20. Is your warranty equivalent to a factory warranty? You want pro-rata protection to TBO, with an initial 6-month, 240-hour non-pro-ratafied satisfaction guarantee. Have them send you a copy of their present written warranty. Read it and see how it compares to the factory's Rare-Metal Medallion warranty; it should stand up pretty well.

CYLINDER HONING: KEY TO LONG TBO

When an engine (or cylinder) fails to break in properly after overhaul, piloting technique generally gets the blame. "You didn't run the engine hard enough," a mechanic is likely to say when an owner brings his engine in for deglazing.

It's certainly true that ring seating depends on high combustion pressures and high piston speeds. But there's more to it than that. Engines sometimes fail to break in even when flown properly, because of factors beyond the pilot's control.

A friend of ours recently came out of top overhaul with his engine (a Continental IO-470) burning over a quart of oil per hour, despite having put the engine in service immediately and run it hard (80 percent power), using straight mineral oil. At 20 hours STOH, the oil consumption still showed no sign of stabilizing (and several jugs were below 60/80 on a differential compression test), so the cylinders were taken off and inspected. An independent expert was called in. He informed our friend of the sad news: the man's barrels had not been honed. (Not only had they not been honed properly—they hadn't been honed at all.)

This is an extreme case, admittedly. But even so, "Improper honing is probably the single biggest reason for break-in problems," a Continental factory engineer told us. "Failure to achieve the proper scratch pattern on the barrel walls is commonplace."

Honing—abrasion etching of the steel barrel to produce a surface that rings can seat to—is normally the last step in cylinder reconditioning, coming after grinding or plating operations. (It also generally comes after valve guide or seat replacement and any welding or stress-relief operations.) Even if no parts are replaced during the top overhaul, standard practice calls for jugs to be honed before being put into service. (Light honing to remove surface varnish is called deglazing.)

Honing is also one of the most operator-sensitive steps in the top-overhaul process—which is another way of saying that the potential for error is high. In aviation, most honing is done by a technician holding a motorized hone/low-speed drill (as opposed to many auto-engine shops in which automated honing machines do the whole job); the technician controls the speed at which the hone is moved through the barrel, and thus the type of scratch pattern produced. The grit-number of the hone, the speed of the hone, the type of lubricant (if a wet honing technique is used), and other factors controlled by the operator, all contribute to the success (or failure) of honing—and subsequent break-in.

After honing, the scratches on the cylinder walls—although not rough enough to feel with your fingernail—will have sharp peaks, with many microscopic tears and folds in the metal. These tears and folds should be removed with 200-grit sandpaper, prior to washing the barrel with soapy water (to remove fine particles).

Continental's honing guidelines (spelled out in Service Bulletin M75-13, Revision 1) are as follows:

"1. Roughen by honing with No. 180 grit stones in a spring-loaded honing head.

Honing is an operator-critical step in the overhaul process. A hand motor and self-centering rotary hone are typically used to give the barrel the specified surface finish.

"2. The bore finish within the piston ring travel should show a cross-hatch pattern produced by a wet honing technique (coolant: 90 percent kerosene, 10 percent oil).

"3. The scratches produced should be crossed and those running in each direction should form an angle of 22 to 32 degrees with the end of the barrel.

"4. Scratches must be uniformly cut in both directions.

"5. The pattern must be clean cut, not sharp, and free of torn and folded metal.

"6. The surface finish of the honed bore shall be 15-30 microinches measured in the direction of piston travel.

"7. Use approximately 200-grit paper and run figure-eights around barrel I.D. to remove small particles of folded and torn metal. As a result, the plateaus should be one-half to two-thirds of the surface.

"8. The surface finish for a distance of .750-in. maximum from each end of the barrel shall not exceed 45 microinches.

"9. Wash the cylinder barrel thoroughly with a brush and hot soapy water to remove any dirt or embedded particles prior to installation."

Note: Lycoming's specified surface finish for ordinary steel barrels is 25-35 microinches; 20-35 microinches for nitrided barrels. (See the *Direct Drive Overhaul Manual*, paragraph 6-105.) Kerosene or light engine oil may be used during a wet honing, according to Lycoming (See Service Instruction No. 1047.)

Chrome cylinders require a little different treatment, since chrome is extremely hard (compared to steel) and does not wear in as fast. Instead of a 180-grit stone, Continental specifies a 280/320-grit aluminum oxide hone stone for final cleanup, with an 80-percent kerosene/20-percent TUL-KUT mixture as lubricant. Continental warns (in S.B. M73-24) not to overhone and not to attempt to introduce heavy cross-hatching in chrome.

If new valve guides or seats are to be installed in a cylinder—or the cylinder is to be subjected to oven-heating for any reason (stress relief after welding, etc.)—honing should be done after, not before, such work. The reason is that honing-oil residue can cook to varnish on barrel walls during oven heating (to remove guides or seats), interfering with later break-in. This fact is noted in a footnote in Continental Service Bulletin M73-24, Revision 1.

Hones for aircraft use (such as Snap-O Tool Co. P/N CF-60C) are spring-loaded (to reduce chatter) and self-centering; thus, they will follow—and not alter—the choked contour of a properly ground aircraft cylinder. Some metal removal is unavoidable, but unless the operator intends to make numerous passes, it shouldn't be necessary to plan on a cleanup allowance of more than a few ten-thousandths'.

After final honing, a soap-and-water wash to remove grit and metal particles is highly recommended. (Particular attention should be paid, in Lycoming engines, to the head-joint nook where the barrel terminates in the head. This space should be cleaned out with a nylon bristle brush and blow-dried with compressed air.) From this point on, fingerprints should be kept off the bare metal, and the cylinder should be put in service as soon as practicable.

Properly honed barrels will have a scratch pattern as shown here, visible to the naked eye but not apparent to the touch. Notice how the crosshatching crisscrosses at an angle of approximately 30 degrees to the base of the barrel.

In its *Direct Drive Overhaul Manual*, Avco Lycoming recommends a buildup oil (for pre-lube of piston grooves, piston rings, etc.) consisting of 15 percent STP ("or equivalent") and 85 percent SAE 50 engine oil. Probably a better idea would be to use straight SAE 50 or 60 mineral oil, however. STP contains an extreme-pressure agent (anti-scuff additive), and some experts feel that EP agents may actually interfere with cylinder break-in. (See SAE Paper No. 810849 by Robert V. Kerley, and *LPM*, March 1984 and November 1983.) The fact is, you want some metal-to-metal scuffing to occur during break-in; the whole purpose of honing is to control the amount of scuffing to just the optimum amount needed for ring seating. If cylinders are overhoned, advanced ring wear will occur (particularly in chromed cylinders); if underhoned, barrel glazing (surface varnish accumulation) will occur, impeding oil control.

You may not be able to exert much control over the honing process directly. But every pilot should know (by looking) how to tell a good hone job from a bad one. And every installing mechanic should know to look carefully at the surface finish of an exchange jug before installing it. There's no excuse for installing improperly honed jugs.

Appendix
EGT
INTERPRETATION

Appendix

EGT
INTERPRETATION

One of the most useful of all cockpit gauges for understanding and troubleshooting firewall-forward problems is the EGT (exhaust gas temperature) gauge. The advent of the EGT—the multiprobe, all-cylinder-display EGT in particular—has meant a revolution in the way pilots monitor, troubleshoot, and operate their engines.

In simplest terms, an EGT system is a "rectal thermometer" for the engine: It puts a *thermocouple probe* (similar in function to a thermometer) inside the exhaust pipe of one, two, or all cylinders; the output is registered in degrees Fahrenheit on a cockpit gauge that can either be analog or digital in design. The gauge reads out the temperature of the exhaust continuously in flight, letting the pilot know, first of all, that internal combustion is indeed occurring, and more important, that it is occurring normally.

The EGT has two uses: One is to enable the pilot to fine-tune his or her mixture management technique (i.e., lean the engine with greater accuracy and self-confidence); the other is to make it possible for the pilot to pinpoint the location—and often deduce the *cause*—of particular mechanical problems. Obviously, an offscale-low indication in conjunction with rough engine operation would mean that a cylinder is cutting out (possibly due to spark plug fouling, valve sticking, or perhaps something more serious). An offscale-high indication, conversely, would be indicative of preignition (a very harmful type of abnormal combustion that can be caused, for instance, by the inadvertent use of jet fuel in place of 100LL).

If the pilot is skilled in the interpretation of EGT readings (and is very familiar with his or her airplane, from years of flying), it is possible to troubleshoot FWF problems of a quite subtle nature—clogged fuel injectors, for example, or drifting mag timing.

To make effective use of an EGT system requires that a pilot know something about the combustion process (since combustion is, directly or indirectly, what an EGT probe measures). Obviously, combustion requires fuel and air—as well as a spark—in order to occur. But the ratio in which the fuel and are present together is fairly critical; not just any ratio will do. After all, when you blow gently on a match, at first it burns faster, because you are supplying a greater flow of oxygen to the fuel (the wood or paper in the match). But if you blow hard enough, the fire goes out—because suddenly the ratio of air to fuel is too great to sustain combustion.

Pilots can control the air-to-fuel, or fuel-to-air (F/A), ratio of their engines by means of the mixture control. Pulling the mixture control out tends to decrease the fuel-air or F/A ratio; enrichening the mixture (pushing the mixture knob in) *increases* the F/A ratio.

The effect of pilot-induced changes to F/A ratio on EGT indications is shown in Fig. A-1. Pulling back the mixture control causes fuel flow to be reduced while airflow through the carburetor is held constant. (In a plane with a fixed-pitch prop, or a turbocharger for that matter, there will in actuality be some changes in airflow as the mixture is retarded; but for purposes of Fig. A-1 we'll assume that the aircraft has a constant-speed prop, so that intake airflow is indeed constant.) The leanest F/A ratios occur on the left-hand side of the graph, while the richest conditions occur on the right-hand side. Exhaust temperature is plotted vertically. In this case, EGT is shown in terms of variation from peak-EGT; but you could just as easily plot "absolute" EGT values (1,200, 1,300, 1,400 degrees F, etc.) along the vertical scale at the top of the graph. The reason actual EGT values are not plotted is that they vary in magnitude from engine to engine, and from throttle setting to throttle setting, whereas variations from peak-EGT are always about of the same magnitude. As plotted, the graph can be considered representative of a wide range of engines.

Notice that as the mixture is retarded, EGT rises in more-or-less straight-line fashion until, at around .067 F/A ratio, the curve peaks and starts back down. The peak-EGT point occurs, as we said, where the fuel/air ratio is such that there is neither an excess of fuel nor of air—all of the reactants are present in the chemically ideal amounts for combustion. Since the throttle setting in this graph is constant, the peak-EGT point represents the F/A mixture at which maximum heat is produced with respect to the amount of air being drawn into the engine. This is *not* the same F/A mixture, however, as that which gives the maximum *power* for the throttle setting selected. Maximum power occurs at about .076 F/A ratio—or 100 to 125 degrees F rich of peak. Why don't peak-EGT and "best power" coincide? The answer has to

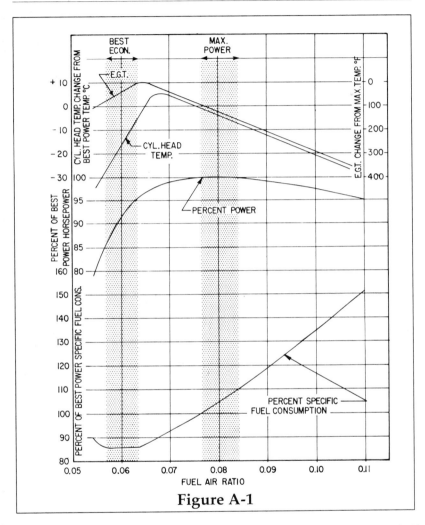

Figure A-1

The relationship of exhaust gas temperature and cylinder head temperature to fuel/air ratio.

do with gas-expansion effects. At a F / A ratio slightly richer than peak, an excess of combustion gases (from incomplete burning of the excess fuel) is produced. These gases, like carbon monoxide, are capable of further oxidation (further burning) to yield a relatively small amount of extra heat energy, but are less dense and therefore take up more space than either their completely burned byproducts or the original fuel vapor. The extra gases produced through incomplete burning thus actually contribute more to piston movement than they would if burned completely to yield a modicum of extra heat. Piston movement, not heat per se, is what results in power; hence "best power" mixture occurs slightly rich of the peak-EGT fuel/air ratio.

The peak-EGT point on the curve, then, can be seen as the mixture that gives the greatest amount of total combustion heat per unit of air (remember, airflow through the engine at a given throttle setting is constant in this example); while on the other hand, "best power" mixture is the F/A ratio giving the most *usable heat* (the most power) per unit of air. This is quite a different thing from getting the most power from a given unit of *fuel*, however. By definition, the best-power-per-unit-fuel mixture would also be the "best sfc" F/A ratio. (Specific fuel consumption, or sfc, is expressed in units of pounds of fuel per horsepower per hour.) The best-sfc point, also known as "best-economy mixture," occurs at or near 0.059 F/A ratio, or about 50 degrees F lean of peak-EGT. Why there? Because as you lean past peak, fuel consumption drops off faster than power production—up to a point. Eventually, as you continue leaning past "best economy" mixture, power production will drop off precipitously (i.e., your engine will cough and quit) even though some fuel is still flowing.

The effect of leaning on airspeed is worth considering. It should be obvious (even though it actually isn't to quite a few pilots) that maximum airspeed comes at *best-power mixture*—about 100 to 150 degrees (F) rich of peak EGT. Any leaning beyond this point will result in a reduction in power and airspeed. How much extra power does "best power" mixture produce over full-rich mixture? Generally speaking, about five to seven percent. Thus, if your plane develops 150 hp in cruise, you can expect to pick up about 10 horsepower by leaning from full-rich to best-power. How much airspeed you pick up depends on the individual airplane, but you can figure on a gain of roughly two and a half percent. So for example, if your plane normally cruises around 150 mph (full rich), leaning to best power will allow you to pick up just under 4 mph—a noticeable increase, just within the limits of measurability.

Some airplanes will actually pick up more than two and a half percent, due to ram effects (the higher the airspeed, the more ram recovery and the better the volumetric efficiency of the engine). The point is, you can lean your engine to "best power" by reference to the

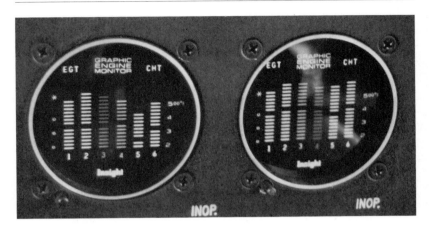

The Graphic Engine Monitor (by Insight Instrument Corp.) gives a bar-stack readout for each cylinder. Each illuminated bar represents 25 degrees of EGT, while a darkened bar represents CHT (as references to a scale on the right). This installation, in a Turbo Aztec, employs one GEM per engine (each one having a probe for every cylinder). The condition of each engine can be ascertained at a glance. When this photo was taken, the left engine's number-five cylinder had just swallowed a valve (note the lower EGT and CHT readings for the fifth bar stack).

airspeed indicator, if necessary (in calm air). The airspeed gain is just large enough to be perceptible to the average pilot flying the average-equipped airplane.

What happens to airspeed if you lean beyond best-power? According to the Cessna 182L owner's manual, a Skylane leaned to 75 degrees rich of peak, rather than 125 F rich, will lose 1 mph in cruise—but will gain a full 10 percent more range (compared to best-power mixture). At 25 F rich of peak, the airspeed loss is 3 mph, but—if Cessna's handbook can be believed—the range increase vis-a-vis best-power is a full 20 percent! (Cessna does not allow leaning beyond 25 F rich of peak, in its 182L owner's manual, citing possible engine roughness due to premature onset of lean misfire in the leanest cylinders of the Continental O-470-R engine.)

Leaning to best-economy provides even more startling gains in range (assuming your engine can be leaned beyond peak without running roughly; many can't). Specific fuel consumption is typically 50 percent higher—yes, 50 percent—at full-rich than at best-power mixture. The ratio of full-rich sfc to best-economy sfc is often 1.7 or better—almost a 2-to-1 ratio. In other words, if your range at full-rich mixture were 600 miles, your range at best-power mixture might be

900 miles; and your range at best-economy mixture might be 1,000 miles or more.

Mixture Maldistribution

Sadly, many general-aviation engines cannot be leaned to best-economy—or even to peak EGT—without running roughly (even at reduced power settings). The reason is mixture maldistribution. Many small-plane-engine intake systems are so poorly tuned that lean misfire begins in the leanest cylinder(s) well before peak EGT is reached in the richest cylinder(s). Hence, arbitrary limits must be placed on leaning, for certain engines (witness Cessna's 25-degrees-rich-of-peak limit for the Continental-powered Skylane).

It's a fact of life that in all but the most carefully designed engines, some cylinders are richer than others. One reason for this is that the distance from the carburetor to the nearest cylinders is often (for large engines, such as the Continental O-470-R) half the distance from the carburetor to the farthest cylinders. Fuel droplets—traveling "uphill" against gravity (thanks to the updraft positioning of the carburetor)—are more likely to reach the near cylinders than the far ones; and the farthest-forward jugs run leanest (in some engines, anyway) as a result. Fuel injection is designed to overcome this limitation. But even fuel-injected engines experience significant inter-cylinder EGT spreads due to nozzle manufacturing tolerances, airflow anomalies, etc.

If you have a multi-cylinder EGT indicator system (a so-called "exhaust analyzer"), it's a fairly simple manner to determine which cylinder is leanest. Your leanest cylinder is the one that reaches peak EGT first as the mixture control is retarded. As you pull the mixture control back in cruise, the EGT indication for each cylinder will initially rise, then fall, in accordance with the pattern shown in Fig. 8-2. Since peak EGT always occurs at or very close to a fuel/air ratio of 0.067, the cylinder that starts out nearest this value will reach peak EGT soonest—and by definition, that's your leanest cylinder.

Pilots often confuse the "leanest cylinder" with the "hottest cylinder." Sometimes the two are the same; but very often, they are not. The cylinder with the hottest peak-EGT indication is not necessarily the leanest cylinder—it may be simply the cylinder receiving the largest total amount of combustants (fuel and air). Remember, it takes air and fuel to make fire, and generally speaking, the more you have of both (together), the hotter the flame. Also, the more compression there is

Single-readout analog-type EGTs (such as this Alcor unit) provide only a fraction of the utility of a multichannel unit such as the GEM. Single-needle units afford an extra measure of precision in mixture control over the traditional "lean it till it misfires" method of leaning, but they are very hard to troubleshoot problems with. For troubleshooting, a multi-display EGT is definitely best.

during combustion, the higher the final temperature (which is another way of saying that your highest-peaking jug may well be the jug with the leak ring and valve leakage—the cylinder with the best compression). It's easily possible, if you think about it, for your richest cylinder to give the highest peak EGT value. The richest jug is the last one to peak. There's nothing that says it can't reach the highest peak. (However, there's nothing that says your richest jug is the one getting the most fuel. It could just as well be the one getting the least air.)

Again: Your leanest cylinder is the one that reaches peak EGT before all the others, as mixture is leaned. The actual magnitude of the peak is of little significance.

A corollary of what we've just discussed is that at any given fuel/air ratio, it's very likely that no two cylinders in your engine will show the same EGT indication. In fact, the difference between the highest cylinder and the lowest cylinder may well be 200 degrees Fahrenheit—or more. This is usually a direct reflection of the effects of mixture maldistribution. In other words, if your engine's intake risers were tuned and of the same length, if your injector nozzles were calibrated to high accuracy, etc., the inter-cylinder EGT spread would narrow, perhaps to zero. And as a result, you could lean your engine more aggressively. As stated above, one of the main limitations to leaning some engines to peak EGT or beyond is the premature onset of lean misfire in the leanest cylinders. Obviously, if every cylinder were equally "lean," you could lean your engine to a further extent before encountering lean misfire. And then the whole engine would just quit (instead of one cylinder)!

In some engines that have a large inter-cylinder EGT spread, it is possible to narrow the gap (and improve mixture distribution) by judicious use of carburetor heat. The improved vaporization of fuel made possible with carb heat aids in "homogenizing" the mixture in carbureted engines, and to a large extent mitigates the problem mentioned earlier of fuel droplets not reaching the distal cylinders (due to airflow problems, and gravity). Bear in mind, however, that carburetor heat—when applied fully—is enormously effective in heating the incoming fuel and air, and the use of full carb heat may cut volumetric efficiency (by reducing density flow). Also, carb heat involves the use of unfiltered air, which means TBO may suffer unless you are flying well above the "dust layer" (which extends to 10,000 feet AGL in certain parts of the country, in summertime). Partial carburetor heat generally does a better job of reducing EGT spread than full-strength carburetor heat; however, the effect varies from plane to plane. As mentioned above, some EGT variations are attributable to differences in ring or valve leakage (compression) from cylinder to cylinder. If this is the dominant problem in your engine, the use of carb heat will not tend to minimize inter-cylinder EGT spread.

Any time you use carburetor heat, by the way, remember that the incoming air—because it is hotter—is less dense, and thus the effective fuel/air ratio is richer. Therefore, you should re-lean any time carburetor heat is used.

Material Limitations

The principal limitations to aggressive leaning or most high-output aircraft engines are material-related. The material properties of iron alloys deteriorate rapidly as the temperature increases above 1,200 degrees Fahrenheit. As tensile strength and hardness go down, wear of moving parts goes up. Also, corrosive attack (always a problem in components exposed to exhaust gases, which are rich in water vapor, acids, and ozone) is accelerated by high temperatures.

Then there is the problem of "creep," which is the tendency of metal alloys to become plastic and flow (or stretch) at very high temperatures. Generally speaking, the creep limit of most austenitic steels is encountered at around 1,400 degrees (it varies for different alloys). Creep properties are given in units of psi loading for a given percentage growth per 1,000 hours. (For low-grade carbon steels, a typical value might be 7,800 psi for 1-percent growth in 1,000 hours.) With the proper engineering handbooks, it is possible to calculate with a pocket calculator how much a turbine blade, or an exhaust valve, will "grow" in 1,000 or 2,000 hours of operation at a given temperature. Just this type of calculation is often used to establish hot-section or major-overhaul TBOs.

The exhaust valves used in modern aircraft engines are usually fabricated not from ordinary steel alloys, but from nickel-based "superalloys" such as Nimonic 80A. These high-nickel alloys provide excellent creep resistance to temperatures of 1,700 F or more. Unfortunately, not every component in an aircraft engine's top end is made of such alloys. (Exhaust stacks are commonly made of 321 stainless, for example, which loses 90 percent of its room-temperature tensile strength at 1,650 F—a temperature easily attainable in many light plane exhaust systems.) Valve guides, in order to provide good wear characteristics, must generally be softer than the valve-stem material designed to run inside them; hence aluminum-bronze and cast iron guides are often specified for aircraft engines.

The point is, many of the metals used in your engine, for one reason or another, are not capable of holding up well under extreme-high-temperature operating conditions, and there's little that can be done about it except to monitor EGT (or TIT) closely, and keep temperatures in check. Fortunately, quite a few of aviation's low-output engines are incapable of producing extremely high EGTs in normal operation. For example, you would be hard-pressed to see EGTs of 1,600 F in a Lycoming O-235-N2C or Continental O-200-A with both mags working, timing adjusted to factory specs, etc. (In fact, leaned to peak EGT in cruise flight, you'd be hard-pressed to see 1,400 F in either of those engines.) Even some high-compression engines, such as the 200-hp Lycoming IO-360-A used in the Mooney 201, are fairly cool-running with regard to EGT. This is not unexpected, since the heating effects of the high compression ratio are usually offset by the (equally high) expansion ratio, which allows exhaust gases to cool before passing the EGT probe. (Here we see yet another subtlety of exhaust analysis, which is that compression ratio and EGT are not necessarily related—something that was first noted by Alfred Buchi in 1909.)

Nevertheless, aggressive leaning can produce valve temperatures (and exhaust-stack temperatures) exceeding 1,400 F in many of today's light plane engines, particularly turbocharged engines. To some extent, Lycoming engines are better protected from heat damage than Continental engines, in the sense that Lycoming exhaust valves are sodium-filled and operate cooler, by a significant margin, than solid-stemmed Continental exhaust valves. Even so, it is a good idea to have a regard for exhaust-temperature limits when leaning an engine—any engine. Not every EGT is calibrated in actual degrees Fahrenheit. Calibrating an EGT system is not difficult, however (Alcor makes an excellent calibrator system; see if your shop has one); and in the long run it will pay dividends to put a red line on your EGT gauge corresponding to 1,650 F (or some lower value).

One of the unavoidable trade-offs of flying is that the more aggressively you lean your engine, the hotter your exhaust components are going to run and the less life they'll have. This is more of a limitation for some engines than for others: Obviously, a 375-hp Continental GTSIO-520-M (with solid-stemmed valves) operating at 30 inches of manifold pressure in cruise will not tolerate the same degree of leaning as a 180-hp Lycoming O-360-A (with sodium-cooled valves) pulling 22 inches in cruise. The GTSIO-520 can be operated the same way, but you'll pay for it in top overhauls (valve jobs) later.

What Does an EGT Probe Measure?

What, exactly, does the EGT probe sense? Obviously it senses exhaust gas temperature, but in a four-stroke-cycle engine, the exhaust valve in any given cylinder spends approximately two-thirds of its time in the closed position. Thus, the EGT probe spends two-thirds of its time sensing—what, exactly? Lack of exhaust gas temperature? Radiant heat from the cylinder head? Nothing at all?

In a multi-probe system, where each exhaust riser has its own "dedicated" probe, you can picture the probe sitting idle two-thirds of the time, then being blasted with a very-high-temperature, high-pressure "pulse" of exhaust gas (which itself is in the process of expanding and cooling). The probe thus is exposed to a regularly recurring cycle of events. The only reason you don't see the needle flicker rapidly on the cockpit gauge is that the combustion cycle is of overall shorter duration than the response time of the probe and needle. The probe itself, after all, has a certain amount of mass, and therefore thermal inertia; and the transfer of heat from a gas to a metal takes time, etc. The point is that what you see on the cockpit gauge is nothing but a rough moving average of the temperature of a certain time-averaged event. It is not an indication of instantaneous exhaust gas temperature.

If the object is simply to have something to lean the engine by, why not just put an automotive-type oxygen sensor in the exhaust pipe and be done with it? (The oxygen sensors used in modern auto emissions

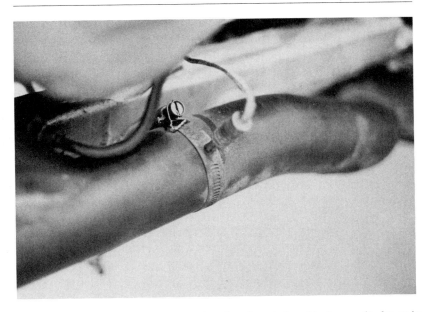

The EGT thermocouple can be mounted in the exhaust pipe of just one cylinder, or in a collector pipe (as here). It reads exhaust temperature more or less directly, thus giving the pilot potentially useful information about the combustion process.

systems actually sense the oxidation potential of the exhaust and therefore permit an a direct determination of fuel/air ratio, without dynamic variations to find a "peak" in the mixture curve.) The answer is that an EGT system gives much more information about combustion than an oxygen sensor ever could. The EGT probe is the engine-maker's equivalent of a medical thermometer—it senses combustion directly (more or less), and therefore gives the operator valuable insights into the combustion process that aren't available by any other means.

Consider the normal combustion cycle: The intake valve opens just as the exhaust valve is about to shut (both are actually open at the same time, briefly; this is known as "valve overlap") and the fuel-air charge is drawn into the cylinder on the piston downstroke. On the compression upstroke, of course, both valves are closed. Ignition occurs at about 20 degrees of crankshaft travel prior to the piston's reaching top center. A flame front spreads outward from each spark plug, and peak combustion pressure is reached very near the crest of piston up-travel. (Peak temperatures reached in combustion are 4,000 F or more.)

Combustion is complete just after the piston starts down, and at around 30 degrees of crank travel before piston bottoming, the exhaust valve opens. Only then does the EGT probe get a "peek" at the leftovers of the combustion process.

Obviously, anything that postpones or accelerates combustion can and will have an impact on EGT, given the sequence of events just described. For example, if ignition timing is shifted early (advanced), so that the spark plugs fire at 30 degrees before top center on the piston upstroke instead of 20 degrees BTC, combustion will go to completion slightly earlier in the cycle than it normally would. As a result, the exhaust gas has more time to cool—more heat is dissipated to the cylinder head—before the EGT probe "sees" what's left. Indicated EGT thus goes down.

Likewise, if ignition occurs late, combustion occurs late and exhaust gases are released earlier in the cooldown cycle than before; hence EGT goes up. This also happens if one spark plug stops firing. Combustion duration is shorter with two flame fronts than with one. Eliminate one spark plug from the combustion event, and peak combustion temperature is reached later than it ordinarily would be; EGT consequently goes up. (Take one magneto off-line, and EGT will go up about 200 degrees for all of an engine's cylinders.)

What happens to EGT when detonation (combustion knock) is encountered? Detonation occurs after spark-plug firing, when the unburned portion of the fuel-air charge ahead of the flame front auto-ignites and explodes all at once (producing the familiar ping or knocking sound). Detonation can be caused by many things: poor-quality gasoline, intake air that's too hot, improperly advanced timing, operating at excessive brake mean effective pressures without proper cooling, etc. Regardless of the cause, however, the effect on EGT is the same: Combustion takes place early, all at once, and heat is released (violently) to the cylinder head and piston. CHT goes up, while EGT goes down. (Notice that CHT and EGT are not always positively correlated. Quite often, as here, they are in fact negatively correlated.)

The mere fact that EGT goes down (as seen in the cockpit) does not necessarily mean detonation is occuring, however, or ignition has drifted early. It may simply mean you've burned a valve, or a bit of carbon is preventing a valve from closing completely, or piston blowby has increased—any of which would reduce compression (and thereby lower the peak combustion temperature). If EGT goes down in all of your cylinders at once, of course, it is unlikely that low compression is to blame. (It's hard to imagine a situation in which every piston suddenly developed excessive blowby, every valve got carboned up, etc.) This is where a multi-probe system proves its worth—if the pilot knows how to interpret it.

Remember, exhaust gas temperature is a reflection of many things: cylinder compression, fuel/air ratio, total fuel and air admitted to the cylinder, combustion duration, valve timing, expansion ratio (the factor by which the exhaust gas is allowed to expand before it exits the combustion chamber), and burn time, to name a few. One reason EGT initially goes up as you lean your mixture is that—all other things being equal—lean mixtures take longer to burn than rich mixtures, and the exhaust gas is hotter when it first leaves the cylinder when the fuel/air ratio is lean.

Many pilot's operating handbooks refer to the EGT gauge as an "economy mixture indicator." It is really much more than that. The EGT is a fabulously responsive tool for "assaying" the combustion process. Spend some time learning its intracacies, and your efforts will be richly repaid, not only in fuel economy, but in maintenance economy as well.

Index